Text Messages received by the author:

"This was a really big help. I speak more goodly now. Thank you."
-R.P., Queens, NY

"I hate learning vocab, but this made it ALMOST fun. Thank you for this."
-Debra K., Manhasset, NY

"Learning new words was almost enjoyable. This is a great method."
-Sasha G., Denver, CO

"I am no longer reticent about appropriating new items in my confabulation. I shall endeavor to imbibe the entire English lexis now. Lol. "
-Simone R., Kings Point, NY

" useful and fun. Great method!"
-Monica G., Jericho, NY

"Improving vocabulary is the single best way to win over people and sound impressive in business. It helps test scores, too. This book does a great job of doing just that."
-Ken Y., SAT Instructor, New York, NY

"I think you made most of these words up and sold them to the people who write dictionaries."
-Ashley H., East Williston, NY

Also by the author:

Professor Dave's Owner's Manual for the SAT – Home Study Edition
Random Scholastic Press (Paperback and e-book) (archaic)

Professor Dave's Owner's Manual for the SAT and ACT Essays
Random Scholastic Press (Paperback and e-book) (archaic)

Professor Dave's Owner's Manual for the SAT – Teacher's Edition (for use in concert
with the Student Workbook) (Paperback) (archaic)
Random Scholastic Press

Professor Dave's Owner's Manual for the SAT – Student Workbook (for use in concert
with the Teacher's Edition) (Paperback) (archaic)
Random Scholastic Press

The Whining Mill (A Novel) (available as paperback and e-book)
Random Scholastic Press

And

Coming soon

Professor Dave's Owner's Manual for the ACT
(Paperback, Student Workbook, Teacher's Edition, and e-books)

Professor Dave's

Owner's Manual for English Vocabulary

The Mnemonic Method

(Home Study Edition)

- Improve Your Vocabulary
  - Proven Techniques
- *Fun!* Vocabulary Retention
  - Live and Web Support
- Accurate Practice Questions For Common Exams

David I Schoen

Independently Published Sponsored by Random Scholastic Press, Bayside, New York

First published by KDP Sponsored by Random Scholastic Press, March 2024.

ISBN-9798878872256

R021924A

Independently published sponsored by Random Scholastic Press, Publishers.

Address inquiries about this and other titles via email to:
inquiries@randomscholasticpress.com

Author's Website:

http://www.thetutormonster.com

New York, NY

Printed in the USA

Professor Dave's

Owner's Manual for English Vocabulary

The Mnemonic Method

© 2024

Thetutormonster.com

Email: <u>tutormonster@gmail.com</u>

This manual is available in two versions:

Paperback

The E-Version – Intended for use on portable devices

David I Schoen

Acknowledgements:

To my students who challenge me by trying to find words in the dictionary that they think I will not know – learning new words by the sneaky method!

To Michel Thomas, author, teacher, hero and mentor who reinvented teaching and learning for me.

To my mother, who made me an avid reader by leaving novels lying around the house, and to my father whose collection of Ellery Queen novels was not nearly large enough. I read them all, dad!

To Strunk and White.

To MAD Magazine – back in the 1970's the magazine included a section called "Wacky Definitions" which was always my favorite. To this day, I still think "bacteria" is the rear portion of a "cafeteria."

To all my students who have come and gone, and the enthusiasm they showed learning new words.

To Baobao, who provides the supportive, fun, loving, and relaxing environment where everything thrives.

Contents

- *The most important thing is to read as much as you can, like I did. It will give you an understanding of what makes good writing, and it will enlarge your vocabulary.*

J. K. Rowling

-*When I wear high heels, I have a great vocabulary and I speak in paragraphs. I'm more eloquent. I plan to wear them more often.*

Meg Ryan

-*You can remember every word to a song that you haven't heard in over 20 years and sing it like it was yesterday. How does that happen? What's the secret?*

Charles T. Bunner

-*One forgets words as one forgets names. One's vocabulary needs constant fertilizing, or it will die.*

Evelyn Waugh

-*Of course, there are big differences in length and character and vocabulary, but each level has its particular pleasures when it comes to the words one can use and the way one uses them.*

Margaret Mahy

Introduction

Welcome to the wonderful world of English vocabulary.

The manual you are reading will help you learn new words. The English language contains over 610,000 words, but no one expects you to learn them all. But learning how words are created is a huge help in deciphering words that are unfamiliar to you. Remembering them afterward is a great challenge. But it can be done.

The English language is strange in many ways. It is one of the few languages that features words with multiple meanings. Furthermore, it has more words than any other language on the planet. This makes for a daunting task vocabulary-wise. Nevertheless, there are methods to the madness.

By learning the construction of the language, we can decipher new words we have never heard before. By remembering associations with these words, we can retain them. How many words in our vocabulary do we use on a daily basis? The New York Times newspaper studied itself a few years back, and do you know what it discovered? A typical daily issue of the newspaper only contains six hundred (600) different words. Surprised? That is typical of the normal vocabulary we use every day. Keep this in mind when studying a new language as well.

Our minds are capable of much more. We retain a stock of words that we rarely use but have instant meaning when we hear them. Have you ever been on an airplane? What is it called when the airplane starts bumping around in flight? Right, turbulence. When is the last time you used the word turbulence? Right. Me either. However, we are able to instantly recall the word and its meaning with no effort when we hear it or need to speak it.

Think again about the word turbulence for a second. Did a memory pop into your head when you thought of the word? Maybe a nasty, stormy flight you took one time on the way to visit grandma. Perhaps you have never been on an airplane but watched a movie in which turbulence was featured. In any case, our minds work in an "associated" way. We associate feelings with words. Smells can trigger memory. Our brains are wired in a strange, wonderful way.

The method for retaining vocabulary in this book takes advantage of how the human brain works. Vocabulary words will be put along with comical (I hope) and memorable sentences that your brain will attach to the words. Some are terrific and memorable right off the bat. Some, not so much. There is room there for you to be creative.

Here is an example:

Let's say you want to remember the state capitals. Not an easy task! If you generate a cute, memorable or funny mnemonic for each one, it is a much *easier* task.

What is the capital of Oregon? Anyone? Oregonians?

The capital of Oregon is *Salem.* So, how do we remember it?

Think of something clever that will help you retain the information. In this case, I think of an *oar*, the wooden or plastic paddle used to move a small boat. *Oar* sounds like the state – Oregon. *My oar is gone.*

What if my *oar* was gone? Then I would have to *sail-em* across the bay. Get the idea? *OARegon, sail-em.* Even if you never open this book again, I promise you will always remember the capital of Oregon: Salem. It works.

Applying this method to English vocabulary is not always easy, but it is always effective. I have done the nasty work for you, generating a mnemonic or memorable definition for each word herein. I have also left space for you to generate your own mnemonic. By doing so, your chances of retaining the words go up exponentially.

Another important and useful tool for remembering vocabulary is to learn common roots of the English language. This manual has an extensive and comprehensive section called *Etymology*, which will introduce you to this concept, or enhance your knowledge of it if you are familiar already. Combine the two, mnemonics and etymology, and you will be a wordsmith in no time.

The words in this manual are grouped into sections that help you remember *synonyms.* Synonyms are words that have similar meanings. By grouping words into blocks that have similar meaning, we have another way to retain information. For reference, the back of the manual has an alphabetical listing of all included words so you can find a specific meaning if you are searching for it.

I've included some easy/medium/difficult vocabulary questions at the end of this manual which were modeled after the old SAT exam that ended in 2015. They're fun, and will challenge your newfound vocabulary. Try them!

Try to absorb everything the manual has to offer. Your speech, writing, and confidence will reflect your efforts.

NOTES

Layout of this Manual

This manual contains several major sections.

First, some background information. We will learn a superb technique for applying our vocabulary. We then dive into the subject of etymology. We will attack the included vocabulary words one by one with mnemonic devices. Finally, there are practice questions designed to hone your skills and practice your newfound knowledge.

Spend a few minutes each day adding new words to your vocabulary. You can make flash cards if you like, but you will find that your retention is exceptional if you use the mnemonic method.

Each word entry contains the word, its part of speech (noun, verb, etc.) and a sample sentence to demonstrate its meaning and usage. Sometimes the mnemonic is the definition sentence, and sometimes it is separate. If you like the mnemonic sentence, great! If not, you can try to generate your own to help you remember the word. Try to add ten to twelve new words each time you open the manual. You will be amazed at how well you remember the words you have studied previously if you use mnemonics.

Please note – the words are listed non-alphabetically in each section intentionally! Most vocabulary books simply list words in alphabetical order, which ends up producing students that know every word beginning with A, but cannot quote an "S" word. This manual does not have that issue, so neither will you. There is an alphabetical listing of all words in the back of the book. Let's get to it.

NOTES

Process Of Elimination

Before we do anything else, let us talk about process of elimination. Keep this concept in mind for *every* multiple choice based test you take in your scholastic life – from the SAT to the AP exams to the MCAT for admission to medical school. It helps on the Bar exam. It helps on that insurance exam your boss wants you to take. Make it your modus operandi.

Process of elimination is based on the concept that the right answer is sitting in front of you, and your chances of choosing it go up exponentially if you *eliminate answers that cannot possibly be correct*. Let me illustrate.

What is the capital of the tiny island nation of Tuvalu?

You didn't even know that was a nation? I assure you, it is. Nice weather, too.

So, what is the capital? I have yet to meet anyone who knows the answer to this question.

Use *process of elimination*. With the answer choices we are given, we can eliminate answers we know are NOT correct, and end up with the right answer. Watch:

3) What is the capital of the island nation of Tuvalu?

(A) Paris

(B) Canberra

(C) Prague

(D) Funafuti

(E) Salem

Got it now? Right, Funafuti. We can eliminate Paris, since most of us know that is the capital of France. Canberra is the capital of Australia. Prague is the capital of the Czech Republic. Salem is the capital of Oregon – you did read that chapter, didn't you? That leaves us with the only possible option – Funafuti. Keep in mind, we are correctly answering a question that we had no idea about going in. See the power?

There are specific marks that you should use to mark up your test booklet. Here are the marks I use for process of elimination.

THE FOUR MARKS OF PROCESS OF ELIMINATION

Ⓐ   **Circled answer. I like this answer. I'm not saying it's definitely right, but I like it. Keep it.**

~   **Tilde (squiggle) Weak answer. I'm not sure, it's kinda ok…but I don't want to eliminate it.**

?   **I have no clue what this word means or what they are talking about.**

/   **WRONG   No good. Done. Gone. Goodbye.**

Every single answer choice should have one of these marks next to it. After you mark up the answer choices, you can choose the *HIGHEST* ranking mark as your answer.

If you have two of the same marks, go back to the question, plug each answer back into the question, and choose.

The Technique for Vocabulary Questions In This Manual

At the end of this manual, you will find interesting vocabulary test questions that are called *Sentence Completion* questions. They're a great way to see your newfound vocabulary in action. Try them! Here's a great technique for ensuring maximum performance.

Effectively mastering *sentence completion* questions is a three step process. Practice it, learn it, master it, and you will improve your reading score.

- **STEP 1** – Cover the answers. Physically take your non-writing hand and cover the answer choices. Do not look at them, they can be deceptive. Do NOT look at them at all. If you're reading them on a screen, do your best to ignore them up front.
- **STEP 2** – Read the sentence, and come up with your OWN phrase, word, or idea for the blank. MAKE SURE IT IS SUPPORTED BY THE SENTENCE, AND ONLY DRAWS FROM THE INFORMATION IN THE SENTENCE. This is the key. Find a word or phrase (does not need to be grammatically correct or even a real word – something that makes sense and is supported by the sentence.) WRITE IT DOWN. ANYWHERE. WRITE IT DOWN. Usually the definition of the blank will appear somewhere in the wording of the question.
- **STEP 3** – Uncover the answer choices, and POE (process of elimination) YOUR word or phrase against the answer choices.

By doing it this way, we ensure we have the correct meaning in the sentence. BE SPECIFIC with your choices. This method avoids the tricky "close" words that are wrong answer choices, and avoids the "it sounds good here" trap that so many people fall into.

Remember, your main goal is to find something that is supported by the sentence. Be a purist. Don't go by feelings, thoughts, ideas – go by WHAT IS SAID IN THE SENTENCE.

Now, learn your vocabulary. There are practice sentence completion questions in the back of this manual along with a review of this technique to ensure your mastery of these questions. You can try some now, or wait until you have enhanced your vocabulary. Practice as many sentence completion questions as you can.

Learning Vocabulary With The Mnemonic Method

Mnemonic (n.) – assisting or intending to assist memory

A mnemonic *device* is a specific sentence, phrase, or idea that contains a meaning. By using mnemonic devices, our brains attach meaning to the phrase. Have you ever listened to a song and realized you knew every word? Did you make a conscious effort to memorize the lyrics? Probably not. Our brains associate the music with the words. The music of the song is acting as a mnemonic device.

We can generate mnemonics as we need them. By generating clever, memorable, funny, or strange mnemonics for vocabulary, we remember the words. It is really that simple.

The difficult part can be generating the mnemonic. I have provided some for the words in this manual. Feel free to generate your own. Ask others for ideas. Whatever method you use to come up with mnemonics, attach something memorable to the word and you will retain the word. Now, I must make a brief disclaimer. Some of my mnemonics stink. Some of them are brilliant. It is not easy to come up with them sometimes, so I encourage you to try your hand at it and invent your own. This will additionally help you remember the words. Writing index cards which include your mnemonic will cement the words in your brain even more.

When you find a new word you do not know, start the process of attaching something memorable to it, and see if you can retain it. Remember in the introduction how I attached *sail-em* to the capital of Oregon? (*The oars are gone – we have to sail 'em.*)

Each word in this manual has a definition and some a separate mnemonic. Try to retain as many as you can. With practice, you will get better and better.

On the following page are steps I recommend you follow. You may develop your own method as well – whatever works for you. The key is to be consistent.

The steps:

1) read the word and read its meaning

2) study the sample sentence to understand how the word is used

3) read the mnemonic and try to "see" it in your mind. If you do not like the mnemonic provided, or it is hard to retain, invent your own

4) review the mnemonic and the words in short chunks – five or six at a time to ensure you remember them

5) make flash cards out of index cards to test your knowledge or have others test your knowledge

Etymology

I have mentioned etymology a few times in this manual, so what is it?

etymology – (n.) – the study of the origin and/or creation of words

Let me begin with an anecdote.

anecdote – (n.) – a brief, personal story told to illustrate a point or idea, usually comical or amusing My aunt Anec always dotes on me and tells me stories.

> *One day, a young college senior went to the office of his college to attend his "graduation review" to ensure he had satisfied his requirements to receive his degree. This is standard procedure at many colleges and universities.*
>
> *The counselor sat him down and explained, rather sheepishly, that he was in fact two credits short of the number needed to graduate at the end of the semester due to course adjustments that were made recently by the administration.*
>
> *"How did this happen?" the student asked, incredulously.*
>
> *"Well," began the counselor, "two of the math courses you took were adjusted from 4 credits to 3 after the fact."*
>
> *"Oh no." The student was upset, confused, and a bit angry. "What the heck am I supposed to do? I don't want to stay another semester!"*
>
> *"Okay, okay, relax." said the counselor. "There is one thing I can recommend. There are several 'half-semester' courses available that you can take and earn the credits you need to graduate on time. "*
>
> *The student glared across the desk at the counselor. As a senior, he was good at college now. His earliest class was at 1:00 PM, three days a week. The concept of adding another class was abhorrent.*
>
> *"Ok, what are my choices?" he asked, resigned to the fact that this was probably the best thing to do.*
>
> *"I do not know offhand, but you should head straight over to the registrar's office and find out. Sorry!"*
>
> *With that, the student got up, shook hands politely with the counselor while calling him horrible names in his head, and walked across the campus to the registrar's office in the administration building.*

Posted on the wall was a list of the 'half-semester' two-credit courses that were available. Of the sixteen listed, only two had available slots. "Oh great." He thought.

The two available 'half-semester' courses were:

Russian Literature

Etymology

The student got on line for the registrar, and considered his choices. Both classes had one thing in common: they began at 7:00AM Monday through Thursday. Yikes. So much for being good at college.

Thinking about the choices, he dreaded taking Russian Literature, but had no idea what the heck etymology was. Study of etys? Huh? He asked a young man behind him if he knew. The young man replied, "Like, I think that's bugs and stuff."

Nope. That's enTomology.

On line in front of our student was this lovely young lady with long hair and a delightful figure. He lost himself in his thoughts as he followed the young lady in the queue up to the registrar's desk. He heard her speak as she reached the front of the line.

"Yes, um," she began in a sing-song voice, "I would like to register for Etymology, please?"

After she had finished, the student winked at her as she walked away, earning him a smile. He turned to the registrar and said, "Yes, Etymology please, here's my student ID." The minds of young men can easily be made up sometimes.

Walking back to his dorm room, he felt a bit better, thinking that no matter what this etymology thing was, at least he would have the lovely young lady to pass the time with.

Let me shorten the story by telling you what happened. First, the young lady never attended the class. Apparently, she had changed her mind or her circumstances had changed. The student? He attended the class. This student completed his bachelor's degree and has gone on to earn two master's degrees us well. So? If you ask him what his favorite course taken throughout his eight years of higher education is, he will tell you: ETYMOLOGY."

He absolutely LOVED the class. From the moment the professor started to speak, he was enraptured. The annoyance of the missing young lady with the long hair was quickly forgotten as the professor began this fascinating course. It goes to show that you never know what new subject will grab your fancy or take you in new directions. Try something new every once in a while, you never know.

So, what is this etymology that so enraptured our young student? **The study of the makeup and origin of words.** Let's take a look.

NOTES

The Origins of English

The English language contains more words than any other language on the planet. It is estimated that the English *lexis* contains more than 610,000 words.

lexis – (n.) the entire word content of a language. "To memorize the entire English lexis would be impossible." My friend Lexis knows every word in the entire language (but she still smells funny).

English is a "borrowed" language – its words are "borrowed" from many sources. Latin, Greek, and French are the cornerstones of the English language.

Modern etymology adds to the language as well. Words are generated by need, by culture, and by commercial application. New words are added to the language every day, some eventually making their way into dictionaries as their usage becomes common and standard.

Consider the word *mouse.*

When I, the author, was in college, you could look up mouse in the dictionary and find this:

mouse (n.) a furry animal of the rodent family. Squeak squeak.

Look it up today. That definition is still there, but it is the *number two* definition. Number one?

mouse (n.) a computer input peripheral intended to be used by the human hand

The word has gone through an *etymological* change due to the advent of the personal computer. Etymology is always changing. Some things, however, stay the same.

NOTES

Roots, Huh! What Are They are Good For?

Learning roots of the English language is a great way to enhance and increase your vocabulary. Since English is borrowed from Latin, Greek, and French, a working knowledge of a few words from these parent languages will help you decipher and reason out the meaning of many English words.

In a few pages appears a list of roots that you should be familiar with. By knowing these roots, you can often figure out the meaning of new words you encounter. Roots stay consistent. Take advantage of this.

For example – the word *phobia* is derived from the Greek word *phobos* which means "fear."

Anytime you see the word *phobia,* it means fear.

The prefix *acro* means "height, or high tip" from the Greek word *akros.*

Think of words you know that contain *acro.* Acrobat. Acrophyte (if you are a bio student.)

An acrobat works in the air. High. An acrophyte is a plant that grows at high altitude. The concept of *high* is contained in the prefix *acro.*

Can you now tell me what you would call a fear of heights?

Right, *acrophobia.* Combine the prefix of *acro (high)* with the word *phobia* and you now have *acrophobia- the fear of heights.* If you know *acro,* and you know *phobia,* you could easily determine the meaning of the word *acrophobia* were you to encounter it while reading or on an exam. That is the power of etymology.

Modern etymology is interesting and useful. Do you realize most of us use the word *Google* as a verb? It may take a few years for dictionaries to add it to their *lexicon,* but I assure you, they will. Make sure you "google" it when it happens.

How about the word *news?*

Years ago, when information dissemination was in its infancy, writers of the brand new things called newspapers searched for a term that would capture the essence of the publication.

Someone suggested making a word that encompassed the four points of the compass. (I love good wordplay.) North, South, East, and West. He took the first initials of the compass points, and created the word – *news.* Information from the four points of the compass. Clever, huh?

Take some time to learn the roots on the following pages, and try to deconstruct words as you encounter them to find their etymological roots. Your vocabulary will benefit greatly. I have included a sample word for each root.

Common Roots Used In English

a-   negative prefix *anaerobic exercise*

ab-   away from/negative prefix *abstract*

ac/acr- sharp *acrid smell*

ad/at- to, toward *attend*

amb-   go/walk *amble along*

ambi-   both/mixed *ambidextrous*

ami/amo- love *amorous relationship*

an/anti against *anti-climactic*

andr-   human, male *android*

anim-   life, spirit *animal*

ante-   before *antechapel*

anthr- human *anthropology*

apt/ept skill, ability *adept*

arbo-   tree *Arbor Day*

arch-   rule, over *Monarch*

aud-   sound *audio*

auto-   self *automatic*

bell/belli- war *belligerent*

ben/bono- good *benefit concert*

bi- two *biannual*

bio/bios- life *biology*

bra- arm *brandish*

carn-   meat, flesh *carnivorous creature*

cent-   hundred *century*

chron- time *chronological order*

circ/circu- around *circumvented*

cide – killing of *homicide*

cis/cise- cut *incision*

clu/clo/cla - close, shut *closet*

co/com/con   with, together *consummation*

contr- against *contrary*

cred-   believe *credence*

culp-   blame *culpable*

cur/cour- run (a course) *course*

de-   away from/opposite, of *detoxify*

dec/deci-ten *decade*

dent-   teeth *dentist*

derm-   skin *dermatologist*

desc-   down *descend*

dext-   dexterity, ability *dexterity*

di-   two, apart, split *diverse*

dic/dict- say, tell *dictate*

dign/dain- worth *dignitary*

digt-   finger, digit *digit*

dis-   apart from, not *disappear*

domi-   rule over *dominate*

dorm-   sleep *dormitory*

dys-   faulty, bad *dysfunctional*

e/ex/ej- out, outward *external*

en/em- into *emissary*

epi-upon *epidermis*

equ/equi-equal *equator*

eu-   good, pleasant *euphemism*

extr-   outside, beyond, additional *extreme*

fac/fic/fig- do, make *figure*

fer/ferr-strong, iron-like *feral*

fid-faithful *fidelity*

fort- strong *fortuitous*

fract- break, split *fracture*

frat-   brother *fraternity*

fren-   highly energetic *frenetic*

gen-   birth, creation, kind, type *generation*

geo-   earth *geography*

gno/kno- know *knowledge*

grand- big *grandiose*

graph- write *calligraphy*

grat-   grateful *gratitude*
gress-   step *progress*
gust-   taste *gusto*
gyn-   female *gynecology*

hemi-   half, split part *hemisphere*
her/hes-stick (on) *hesitate*
herb-   plant *herbivore*
hetero- different, mixed *heterosexual*
hex/sex- six *hexagon*
homo-   same *homosexual*
hyd/hydr-water *hydroplane*
hyper- over, beyond *hyperactive*
hypo-   under, insufficient *hypothermia*

il-   not *illegal*
im-   not, into *impossible*
in-   not, into *intolerable*
inter-   between *international*
intra-   within *intrastate commerce*
itis-   inflammation, infection
dermatitis
ium-   place, building of *gymnasium*

jaun-   yellow *jaundice*

lab/labo-work *labor*
laud-   praise *applaud*
lav-   wash *lavatory*
lev-   rise *levitate*
log/loqui-to speak *loquacious*
lu/luc/lum-light *luminary*

mag/magna-   great *magnificent*
mal-   bad *malevolent*
man/manu-hand *manuscript*
mar/mer-sea *mermaid*
matr-   mother *matriarch*
met/meter measure *thermometer*
meta   more, beyond *metaphysics*
mic/micro-   tiny *micrometer*

mill-   thousand *millimeter*
mis-   wrong, bad *misunderstand*
mit-   send *mitigate*
mob/mobi-moving *mobile*
mor/mort-death *mortified*
morph-change (shape) *anamorphic*
mut-   change, alter *mutation*

nat/natu-natural, birth *nature*
neg-   negative *negate*
neo/nov-new *novel*
noct-   night *nocturnal*
nom/nym-name *synonym*
non/not-negative prefix *non-negotiable*
nounce-call *announce*
nox/nec-harmful *noxious*
nym – name, label *pseudonym*

ob-   against *obstruction*
olfac-   smell *olfactory*
ology- study of *geology*
omni-   all, every *omnipotent*
ory-   place of *dormitory*
pac/pax/plac-   peace, pleasing *pacify*
pan   all, everywhere *pandemic*
par   equal *parallel*
para-   beyond *paranormal*
path-   feeling, emotion *empathy*
patr-   father *patriarchal*
pen/pend-weight *stupendous*
pent-   five *pentagon*
peri-   around *periscope*
phil-   love, high regard *philosophy*
phob-   fear *pyrophobia*
phon-   sound *phonics*
pod/ped-foot *pedestrian*
ped – child *pedophile*
pon/pos-place, put, pose *position*
port-   carry *airport*
post-   after *post-traumatic stress*
poten- power, influence *potential*

pre-   before *precede*
pro-   for *progress*
prox-   near *proximity*
pseudo-false *pseudonym*
pug-   fighting *pugnacious*

quad-   four *quadrant*
qui-   quiet *acquiesce*
quint-   five *quintessential*

re-   again *redo*

schi-   split *schism*
sci/scien -knowledge *science*
scop-   see *telescope*
scrib/scrip-write *script*
sec/sequ-follow, come after *sequential*
sed/sid-sit, be still *sedentary*
solo-   alone *solitary*
son/soni-sound *supersonic*
soro-   sister *sorority*
spec/spic-see, look *speculate*
sta/sti- still, unmoving *stationary*
sua-   smooth *suave*
sub-   under *subway*
sui – self *suicide*

super- beyond, greater than *superhuman*
syn/sym -bring together *symphony*
tact-   touch *tactile*
tech/techn-tools *technology*
tele-   at a distance *telephone*
temp-   time ten/tend- hold *temporary*
terr-   earth, ground *territory*
tox-   harmful, poisonous *toxic*
tract-   pull *tractor*
trans-   across *trans-Atlantic*
trep-   fear, anxiety *trepidation*
tri-   three *tricyle*

un-   not *unsanitary*
uni/uno- one *unicycle*
us/ut-   use *useful*

val/vale-value, feel *valor*
vend-   sell *vendor*
ver/vera/veri- true *verify*
verge-   boundary, together *converge*
verse-   turn *traverse*
vi/vit/viv- alive *vivid*
vid/vis-see *vision*
voc-   call, talk *vocabulary*
vor- eat, consume *voracious*

NOTES

How to Deconstruct and Use Etymology

Now that you have seen a few roots and learned about the construction of English, how to you put this into practice?

When you encounter a word you do not know, look for familiar roots to see if you can discern the meaning of the word. Anything found may help determine the word – or it may help you *eliminate* the word from consideration.

Let's look at a few examples.

siblicide

What the heck is siblicide?

Is there anything in the word that you recognize? Yes. I know the suffix (ending) *cide* means *killing. (homicide, suicide, pesticide)*

Can you think of a word that includes the letters *sibli?*

How many of you thought of *sibling?*

A sibling is a brother or a sister. Can you guess what *sibilicide* means?

Right. The killing of one's own brother or sister. Terrible thought, but great use of etymology.

How about a favorite subject of students everywhere: *geography*

A simple yet elegant etymological construction. Can you pick it apart?

geo – earth *graph* – write

Therefore, *geography* must be something about writing about the Earth. That is exactly what it is.

Practice this technique and you will enhance your skill rapidly. A quick disclaimer – not *all* English words will conform to this. Occasionally words have hard-to-trace etymological sources or they will have mutated over time to mean other things (remember mouse?) You will find most words are easily dissected using etymological knowledge. It is a great tool.

Yes, These Really Are Words:

English is a strange animal. Here are some words you may not believe ARE words, but I assure you, they are.

furthermore – to say "and another thing.."

I am not going to the movies; furthermore, I'm not going to dinner either!

heretofore – before this time; until now, previously

This was something heretofore not mentioned.

hereinafter – afterward in this document or statement

We shall refer to him as "the man" hereinafter.

inasmuch – because, contraction of "in as much"

I won't go fishing inasmuch as I hate the water.

insofar – to such an extent; as possible

I will do the paper insofar as I can.

likewise – the same; in addition to

I am going to start working out – you should do likewise.

moreover – in addition to what has already been presented

He is a great singer; moreover, he can play a mean piano too.

nevertheless – however; in spite of that; even though

I want the new car; nevertheless I'm going to save my money and hang on to this one for a while.

nonetheless - however

Nonetheless, you had no reason to hit him.

notwithstanding – in spite of the fact that

His actions notwithstanding, you should not have pushed him in the pool.

ought – should

You ought to be sleeping by now.

ongoing – continuing

They have maintained an ongoing relationship for decades.

therefore – as a result of

The cat was unhappy; therefore, he scratched me.

thereby – by the means of

I washed the windows thereby allowing me to see the outside world.

whereas – while on the contrary

He is a nice person whereas his wife is mean.

whereby – by what or by which

This is the way whereby you can reach the cabin.

Just For Fun

Studying should not be all drudgery – just be sure you remember these are NOT the real definitions…

Wacky Definitions (Or – the purification of English)

aibohphobia – fear of palindromes

bacteria – rear portion of a cafeteria

baroque – what you are when you run out of Monet

broadband – an all-female musical group

buffet – a French word that means "get up and get it yourself"

bulldozer – a device used to make male cows go to sleep

coral – where sea-horses are kept

defeated – chopped off at the ankles

deforestation – refusing to watch the movie, "Forrest Gump."

diplomat – a person that can tell you to go to hell in such a way that you actually look forward to the trip

eclipse – what a barber does for a living

fission – an outdoor sport favored by nuclear scientists

girafitti – uninvited writing or painting on a building done very high up

hence – the enclosure around a hen coop

impeccable – unable to be eaten by a chicken

intense – where people sleep when they go camping

justice – a decision in your favor

knapsack - a sleeping bag

lemonade – a benefit rock concert to help citrus growers

lexicon - putting Lexus stickers on a Toyota to fool others

mortician – engraver

opera – when a man is stabbed in the back and instead of bleeding he sings

oregano – the ancient Italian art of pizza folding

parasites – what you see from the top of the Eiffel Tower

polaroids – What Eskimos suffer from when they sit on the ice too long.

purranoia – fear that your cat is up to something evil

recursive – see "recursive"

shin – device for finding furniture in the dark

speculate – the state of having your eyeglasses delivered after the promised time

textspectation – the anxious feeling one gets awaiting a reply to a text message

upgrade – taking old problems out, putting new problems in

vegetarian – ancient Native American word for "lousy hunter"

will – dead giveaway

zinc – where you wash ze zaucepans

A Few Awesome Etymological Constructions

Here are some of my favorite etymological constructions. How many can you figure out before reading the description?

vaccine (n.) any preparation used to prevent disease by triggering the body's immune response

Etymology – from the Latin *vacca*, meaning cow – the story goes as such: A doctor in the late 1800's noticed that women who had come in contact with cowpox were much less likely to contract smallpox. Smallpox could devastate entire communities, so this was an important realization. By exposing as many people as possible to cowpox, which was harmless to humans, the rate of contraction of smallpox was greatly reduced. Hence, the word vaccine tributes its cowlike beginnings.

clue (n.) anything which serves to guide or direct toward the solution of a problem or issue

Etymology – from the Old English "clew", which meant a ball of yarn or thread". In Greek Mythology, a ball of yarn was helpful in finding the way out of a maze. Thus, a "clue/clew" will help you find the solution to a problem.

plumber (n.) a craftsman specializing in piping, water movement and management, and installation and repair of sinks, toilets, and other water related paraphernalia.

Etymology – from the Latin for lead, plumbum, as referenced in the Period Table of the Elements as well, PB. The earliest plumbers worked with lead pipes primarily, which led to the name of the craftsman – plumbers.

butcher (n.) a craftsman who prepares animals as food

Etymology – from the old French *bochier*, which meant *slaughter of goats*. From that, it's easy to see how the modern usage came to be.

tycoon (n.) a person of great wealth or influence

Etymology – This word comes to English by way of the Far East, from Japan. *Taikun*, which has roots in the Chinese language, means "great ruler." Original traders to the Far East slightly misinterpreted the word as meaning a king, or other ruler. But as economic power ruled the day at the time, tycoon meant "powerful, wealthy, in charge" as it does today.

boycott (n.) a group effort to abstain from or prevent dealings with a business or individual for the purpose of intimidation or coercion.

Etymology – Another example of how English can be difficult. Roots won't help here, unless you know there was a man named Boycott! Boycott was a property manager for an absentee landlord who got into a heated dispute with a group of farmers. The farmers organized and refused to pay rent, which eventually led to Boycott's replacement by the landlord. A term was born.

nicotine (n.) a liquid alkaloid found in tobacco

Etymology – Named for the French diplomat Jean Nicot. Nicot is credited with bringing the first tobacco plants to France.

antidisestablishmentarianism (n.) opposition to the withdrawal from mainstream society, originally from the Anglican church in England in the 1800's.

Etymology – This one is just downright pretty.

anti – against   dis – not   establishment – mainstream, normal, regular societal norms   tarian – one who   ism – the act of following

Used a lot in the 1960's, attacks on the "hippies" of the day were organized into efforts to bring them "back into the fold." Teams of trained therapists were hired to "go against those who went against mainstream society." How cool is that

Vocabulary Words
How These Words are Organized

Each entry in the list is organized as follows:

- Categorized by general meaning or type
- Word
- Part of speech (noun, verb, adjective, adverb of *primary* use)
- Brief definition
- Sample sentence (mnemonic or informative in nature)
- Mnemonic to remember the word (if separate from the definition sentence)

Study a few every time you sit down with this manual. Learn a few per day. Make flash cards if you wish, but be sure to include all of the elements above on your flash cards. Get creative with your vocabulary! Get creative with your mnemonics. Enjoy.

The words are organized by category, alphabetically within that category. A complete alphabetical list of all words appears in the back of this manual.

NOTES

Amounts

rescind (v.) to take back, repeal as in a rule or policy *The company rescinded the rebate offer when it realized the price had been advertised incorrectly.* Rather than RESEND it, they decided to RESCIND it.

curtail (v.) to reduce or lessen *In an attempt to curtail my spending, I took a smaller apartment.* Cut off the TAIL to make it smaller.

accretion (n.) slow growth *The accretion of many years has made my bank account grow.* To secrete is to ooze, to ACCRETE is to grow.

amalgamate (v.) to combine, unite *His diplomatic manner allowed him to amalgamate the normally feuding groups.*

preponderance (adj.) best in importance or quantity *The United States' preponderance in air power is fascinating.*

penultimate (adj.) second to last *On our penultimate day of vacation, we went diving since we could not dive on the same day we were to fly.*

increment (n.) an enlargement; the process of increasing by small pieces *He made the portrait larger incrementally; he added little bits to each edge.*

abridge (v.) amending to make shorter *My first novel was too long so I abridged it. The poorly designed ABRIDGE was too short to reach the other shore!*

profuse (adj.) lots of, plentiful *The profuse cheers rang out as the team entered the field. Pros fused from the players.*

copious (adj.) lots of *On a clear night away from the city lights, the stars above are copious to the eye.*

cumulative (adj.) increasing, building upon itself, growing larger *The cumulative effects of the lack of sleep were apparent – he looked tired and beat up.*

ubiquitous (adj.) everywhere, widespread *Dogs are ubiquitous in the United States, as there are an estimated 70,000,000 dogs in the country.*

pervasive (adj.) getting everywhere, omnipresent, having a tendency to seep everywhere *When we arrived at the Hershey factory, the pervasive smell of chocolate was hard to ignore.*

extraneous (adj.) irrelevant, extra, not necessary, non-essential *The report turned out to be extraneous as we had all the information we needed already.*

medley (n.) mixture of differing things *His record collection featured a medley of genres from rock to Beethoven symphonies.*

rife (adj.) full of, containing a large amount of   *It was ironic that the grammar guide was rife with grammar errors.*

discrepancy (n.) difference between expected and actual amount *The bank's statement and my records showed a vast discrepancy.*

abate – (verb) to lessen, reduce *After pouring for hours, the rain abated.* The fish ate all ABATE, we had none left.

aggrandize (v.) to increase *He always left his phone book out to show the celebrities he knew – in this was he aggrandized his stature.*

augment (v.) to add to, expand, make larger *She felt her book collection was too small, so she went to an auction to augment it.*

ephemeral (adj.) short-lived, fleeting, brief *She promised to cook for me every night, but her promise was ephemeral.*

Awesome!

ardent (adj.) passionate, emotional *His ardent support of the team was obvious because every article of clothing he owns has the team's logo on it.* Let's go Ardents!

ebullient (adj.) extremely lively and happy, enthusiastic *She was ebullient accepting the award; she had waited for this moment her whole life.*

avid (adj.) excited about, enthusiastic about *His avid interest in aviation led to him obtaining a pilot's license.* The avid aviator.

zealous - (adj.) wanting desperately, ambitious *He was zealous about getting the promotion, so he worked 12 hours a day.* I'm so ZEALOUS because I'm JEALOUS. I want it.

fervent (adj.) passionate, very into *He was a fervent supporter of the politician – he spoke about him all the time.* Fervent for president.

intrepid (adj.) brave in the face of trouble or danger *The intrepid police officer was decorated for his bravery.*

effervescent (adj.) bubbly, lively, friendly *His effervescent manner affects everyone he meets; he makes people smile.*

fanatic (n.) one with intense enthusiasm for something *He was a football fanatic; for he sat in front of football games for twelve hours every Sunday.*

exuberant (adj.) very excited, extremely happy *His exuberant manner was contagious; he had us all excited to go after a few minutes.*

vibrant (adj.) enthusiastic, exciting, lively *The vibrant colors of the room were amazing.*

fortitude (n.) strength, guts, bravado *Hercules was a pillar of fortitude.*

cosmopolitan (adj.) sophisticated, worldly, well-travelled *We were fascinated listening to the cosmopolitan musings of the man in the restaurant.*

pulchritude (n.) physical beauty or attractiveness *She is the embodiment of pulchritude; she is lovely and graceful.*

divine – (adj.) godlike, extremely great or wonderful *This dessert is simply divine.* The fruits of DEVINE are incredibly good!

paradigm (n.) a perfect example *He was the paradigm of the piano student – practicing daily and mastering his assignments.*

archetypal (adj.) a superb or very typical example of something *The dark, greasy-haired man was the archetypal villain.*

adept (adj.) extremely skilled *Michael Jordan was one of the most adept players to ever take to the basketball court.*

deft (adj.) skillful, adept, very capable *Charlie was adept at making a superb pot of coffee after working in Starbucks for a few months.*

confection (n.) a sweet snack or treat *The chocolatier offered an incredible array of confections.*

resilient (adj.) bounces back easily from bad happenings *The company showed great resilience – despite stiff competition it came out on top in the rankings.*

pinnacle (n.) the very top *His new novel, The Whining Mill, reached the pinnacle of the bestseller list very quickly.*

ornate (adj.) elaborate, excessively decorated *Upon our arrival at the mansion, we were shown into an ornate sitting room.*

crescendo (n.) a steady increase in intensity or volume *This definition is reaching its*
crescendo!

paramount (adj.) super-important *Fixing the economy was the paramount business of the new leader.*

Bad Behavior

cavort (v.) to leap around, behave boisterously or wildly *While we enjoyed the sunset, the children cavorted on the beach.*

façade (n.) a phony appearance or attitude *Although he was hurt by badly, he maintained the façade of being in high spirits for our benefit.*

incessant (adj.) repeating to the point of annoyance *His incessant drumming kept us up nights.*

irascible (adj.) nasty, easily angered *His irascible personality caused him to get into many fights others would have avoided.*

puerile (adj.) childish, immature *The puerile child was finally removed from the church by his mother.*

infamy (n.) extreme notoriety, evil fame *Al Capone, gangster, will forever live in infamy.* President Roosevelt, referring to December 7, 1941. "A day that will live in infamy…"

boisterous (adj.) loud and full of energy *The boisterous crowd drowned out the sound of the music from where we were sitting.*

demagogue (n.) a leader who appeals to a people's shortcomings, desires, or prejudices *The candidate was an obvious demagogue; he blamed immigrant workers for the lack of jobs at home.*

toady (n.) one who flatters in the hope of gaining favors *The manager's gopher was such a brown- noser that we referred to him as the 10th-floor-toady.*

larceny (n.) stealing or theft *I convinced my sister that stealing my pretzels was grand larceny, punishable by 25 years in prison.*

nefarious (adj.) evil and villainous *Stewie from Family Guy is the most nefarious baby I have ever seen portrayed.*

malevolent (adj.) evil, having evil intent *The malevolent teenager put broken sticks on the skate path hoping to trip skaters that happened by.*

impudent (adj.) casually rude, impolite *His impudent comment to the Queen earned him an overnight visit to the dungeon.*

gluttony (n.) overeating or drinking *His gluttony led to him needing a new wardrobe – two sizes bigger! If you engage in GLUTTONY, you won't be able to close the BUTTONY*

brusque (adj.) short of manner, abrupt, dismissive, rude *The pilot's brusque manner offended some of the passengers.*

deride (v.) to laugh at mockingly, make fun of *The nasty student derided the foreign student's accent. "You wan to go for deride?"*

accost (v.) to verbally confront, argue with *Normally calm and cool, Sheryl accosted the waiter when he spilled her drink for the fifth time.*

denigrate (v.) to insult or belittle the opinion of *Rather than denigrate his opponent, the gubernatorial candidate took the high road in his ads.*

devious (adj.) deceitful in an evil, intentional way *Saying the dog ate my homework was a devious plan, and it didn't work.*

pernicious (adj.) destructive or harmful *The hurricane had a pernicious effect on the city – it would be remembered for generations. Pernicious is vicious.*

avenge (v.) to seek revenge *He vowed to avenge the person who stole his essay.*

sophomoric (adj.) immature, juvenile *His childish behavior made him seem sophomoric in our eyes.*

complicit (adj.) being a partner in a crime or bad act *He was complicit in her bad behavior – he knew she was cheating on her boyfriend but said nothing.*

concoct (v.) to come up with a story, make up *The professor did not believe the story he concocted as to why he was late.*

ChChChChCHanges

mutable (adj.) able to change (Because fashion is so mutable, what is trendy today will look outdated in five years.)

coalesce (v.) to form into a whole from different parts *The singers coalesced nicely into a choir group.*

refract (v.) to distort, bend, change *Prisms refract light, bending it through its mass which produces a display of the colors of the spectrum.*

congeal (v.) to thicken into solid form, usually through spoilage *Something we left in the fridge all summer had congealed into something unrecognizable.* Like GEL, congeal is a solid liquid.

abrogate (v.) to do away with (usually by those in position of power) *When due process is abrogated in society, chaos reigns.* A – bro – hit the gate, leave!

innovate (v.) to do something in an new or unusual way *Technical innovations for automobiles have made for more dependable, safe transportation.* To do something new, you must be INNOVATIVE – LIKE CREATIVE.

defunct (adj.) no longer used or around *The defunct movie theatre was converted into a nightclub.* It no longer functions – it DEFUNCTions.

catalyze (v.) to charge up, inspire *The union delegate's speech catalyzed the membership.* Do not paralyze, simply CATALYZE.

proclivity (n.) a strong tendency or attraction toward something *Weird as it sounds, Peter's childhood proclivity for torturing small animals grew into a desire to become a surgeon.*

dynamic (adj.) changing constantly or actively *The city's theatre offerings were quite dynamic; a new show seemed to open every week.* If you want to CHANGE something, use DYNAMITE its DYNAMIC.

inure (v.) to make accustomed to, to get used to *Flying airplanes for years makes one inure to turbulence and heights.* I'm used to it – so it's INURE face – it won't bother me. INURE – won't bother me.

malleable (adj.) shapeable, bendable *Pure gold is so soft it is malleable with the bare hands.* I can bend the MALL.

wane (v.) to become smaller, dwindle *As he realized how silly the whole thing was, his anger began to wane.* My friend WAYNE is SHRINKING.

modulate (v.) to move from one state (virtual) to another, especially in music *His symphony modulated several times from one key to another.*

mercurial (adj.) changing quickly in attitude or action *We could never decide on a restaurant, for she was so mercurial we would be discussing twenty different choices in a manner of minutes and she could never choose one.*

protean (adj.)capable of changing shape; containing many varieties *Roger's protean abilities included flute playing and baseball pitching.* PROTIENS change shape.

anesthesia (n.) loss of sensation *The dentist used anesthesia to put me out when he pulled my teeth.*

immutable (adj.) cannot be changed or modified *Time is immutable and constant.* My stereo's iMMUTable button is broken; I cannot change the volume.

fickle (adj.) changing in character frequently, capricious *My fickle friend can never decide what he wants, then when he does, changes his mind two seconds later.*

C'Mon, You Lazy Bum

lethargic (adj.) sluggish or apathetic *His lethargic attitude led to him being late on every project.*

indolent (adj.) lazy *I love the word indolent; it makes my laziness seem classy.*

soporific (adj.) causing sleep, making sleepy *The sophomore was put to sleep by the soporific lecture.*

languid (adj.) slowed in manner from tiredness or weakness *After our long hike on the hot day, I was languid and very thirsty.*

sedentary (adj.) sitting around a lot, lazy *The sedentary student does not do well in school.*

lassitude (n.) tiredness from poor health or too much work *He used his lasso so much he suffered from lassitude.*

sluggish (adj.) slow moving, dragging *I was so sluggish Monday morning I was late for the train.*

torpid (adj.) lethargic, dormant, lacking motion, lazy *Usually active, the dolphin was torpid in the pool, basking in the sun.*

stagnate (v.) to remain inactive, not moving *His career in middle-management stagnated his career – he had nowhere to go.*

furtive (adj.) secretive, sly, sneaky *Hiding money in your sock is not a furtive move, it just makes the money stinky.*

culpable (adj.) deserving blame *Someone shouted, "Mia Culpa!" which, in Latin, means, "My fault." But I don't speak Latin.*

discursive (adj.) not in order, randomly arranged, haphazard *The speech was so discursive we forgot what he was talking about all together.*

facile 1. (adj.) easy, requiring little effort, or superficial, not deep (depending on context) *His facile treatment of the game led to a short, quick victory for its players.*

flaccid (adj.) limp, not firm *The weather was so hot the plants outside became flaccid from lack of water.*

obtuse (adj.) not quick or sharp in intellect, slow, dull *His obtuse manner led to many people taking advantage of him.*

deter (v.) to discourage, prevent from doing *He could not deter her from going on the trip with Jeter.*

Decisions

capitulate (v.) to surrender, to give in *Joe bugged his boss for a raise every day for a month until he finally capitulated.*

meticulous (adj.) extremely careful *Fine watches are assembled meticulously.*

adorn (v.) to decorate *He adorned himself with necklaces and bracelets.*

cajole (v.) to urge *Lexie's friends cajoled her to come out for the night.*

preclude (v.) to prevent *His weight precluded him from getting on the ride, he was simply too big.*

agnostic (adj.) believing that God's existence cannot be proven or disproven *Although he was agnostic, he attended church every Sunday out of respect for his parents.*

consumption (n.) the act of using or eating *The consumption of fossil fuels increases every year worldwide.*

coagulate (v.) to thicken, to clot *Mom's chicken soup is best the second day, after it has had a chance to coagulate overnight.*

discomfit (v.) to ruin the ease of, to confuse or baffle *When all his daughters were crying at once, they discomfited their father like never before.*

carouse (v.) to party *We caroused for hours after the performance.*

apprehend 1. (v.) to seize, arrest, grab *The thief was apprehended after a brief chase.*

emulate (v.) to imitate or copy *He emulates Bill Bruford when he plays the drums, and it's not a bad imitation.*

expunge (v.) to completely destroy, get rid of *The judge was willing to expunge his bad record in light of his heroic actions.*

negligent (adj.) careless, neglectful *Leaving the car door unlocked in the bad neighborhood was a negligent thing to do.*

abduct – (verb) to take a person by force, kidnap *The wealthy merchant was abducted and held for ransom.* He was hidden in the abDUCT by the kidnappers.

foil (v.) to beat or thwart, frustrate, defeat *The plan was foiled by the police, and the robbers were captured.*

ascertain (v.) to get, to learn *We were able to ascertain his whereabouts by using an internet search engine.*

collusion (n.) secret conspiracy, hidden agreement *Working in collusion, the robbers scoped out the vacant house.*

abet – (verb) to help or aid *The loud storm helped to abet his escape.* His finances were aBETTED by his successful gambling.

insinuate (v.) to suggest indirectly or subtly, to hint at *When he stated "no one else was home" he was insinuating that I was responsible for the broken vase.*

abide (v.) to put up with, tolerate *We decided to abide by his decision.*

beseech (v.) to beg strongly *The pilot beseeched the tower to clear all runways for his emergency.*

abjure (v.) to reject or renounce *To demonstrate his kindness, the new king abjured the policies of the former monarch.*

pillage (v.) to seize or plunder, especially via attack *The pirates pillaged each town they visited.*

circumvent (v.) to go around or get around *The students learned to circumvent the dress code by wearing long jackets whenever teachers were around.*

Descriptions

iridescent (adj.) containing all the colors of the rainbow, showing rainbow colors *Her iridescent diamond glistened in the sunlight.*

inchoate (adj.) formless or shapeless, in the beginning stages *The new management at the company is inchoate, as the former leaders were all replaced at once.*

nocturnal (adj.) pertaining to nighttime *Owls are nocturnal creatures, rarely seen during daylight.*

staid (adj.) serious of attitude, countenance, or manner. *The staid guards of the Tower of London never change their facial expressions.*

incisive (adj.) clear, direct, to the point *His incisive comment brought the whole picture into focus.*

partisan (n.) a follower, one who goes along with the position of the party or company *The governor never made up his own mind, for he always voted along partisan lines.*

rash (adj.) hasty, quick to act without pre-planning *Because he was so rash, he ran into the woods without looking. Later, from poison ivy, he developed a RASH.*

docile (adj.) easily trained, calm *The docile parrot went with his owner everywhere.*

animated (adj.) lively, upbeat, full of energy *Geo gets very animated when he talks about guitar players.*

renown (n.) honor, acclaim, fame *A renown author, it will be hard for J. K. Rowling to follow up the Harry Potter series.*

cursory (adj.) brief to the point of only scratching the surface, not looking deeply into *He took only a cursory glance at his familiar schedule.*

luminous (adj.) brightly lit or glowing *The luminous garden was a sight to behold.*

laudatory (adj.) praiseworthy, great, really cool *The laudatory comments from the critics gave him the courage to write another book.*

latent (adj.) hidden, but could out at any time, lying in wait *Dave's latent obsession with chocolate had us hiding our candy stash constantly.*

novice (n.) a beginner, one with little training or experience *A novice martial artist, he pulled many muscles trying to do too much too soon.*

cerebral (adj.) brainy, smart, intellectual *The scientists attempt at a novel was too cerebral, I mean, who "pickles their liver in alcohol?"*

feral (adj.) wild, undomesticated *We have several feral cats in our backyard; they will not let anyone approach them.*

reclusive (adj.) liking to be alone, like a hermit *No one could reach the reclusive author to get an interview about his new book.*

acute 1. (adj.) sharp, accurate, intense *The acute pain in my foot made walking very difficult.*

amorphous (adj.) without shape *The amorphous blob that appeared on my window turned out to be the shadow of my teddy bear on the floor!*

ballad (n.) a love song, a slow song *You Belong To Me is a beautiful, slow ballad.*

antiseptic (adj.) clean, sterile *The antiseptic room demonstrated his obsessive personality – there was not a speck of dust to be found.*

circumspect (adj.) cautious *The Marines were circumspect approaching the enemy position.*

aquatic (adj.) of or pertaining to water *The aquatic theme of the Princess Resort is breathtaking.*

cowardice (n.) fear of action; self-doubt; lack of confidence *The lion was so filled with cowardice, he ran from the little bird.*

Desires, Wishes, and Wants

accede (v.) to agree to *When my sister wanted to cook lasagna instead of turkey, I reluctantly acceded.*

amorous (adj.) showing passion and/or love *When I see her, I get an amorous feeling.*

insatiable (adj.) incapable of being satisfied *She had an insatiable desire for chocolate; she simply couldn't get enough.*

compliant (adj.) willing to go along with, agreeable *The girls were compliant when their friends made plans for the outing.*

covet – (verb) to intensely desire someone else's belongings *He coveted his neighbor's new sports car.* I COVET that cover, it should be mine!

wanton – (adj.) undisciplined, rude, lustful *His wanton appetites brought him much trouble.* Wanton soup is evil! It leads to rude, lustful behavior! Evil wanton soup.

wistful – (adj.) full of yearning, desiring, wanting *He had a wistful expression on his face as he watched her walk away.* Wishful- wistful – same thing.

whimsical – (adj.) light-hearted, fanciful *The young whimsical girl loved to pretend she was a fairy princess.*

emote (v.) to express emotion or feeling *He was such a talented actor he could emote any feeling with ease and make the audience believe it.*

covet (v.) to strongly desire somethings of another's *My neighbors Jaguar is something I truly covet.*

cupidity (n.) strong desire, love (usually with a negative flavor) *His cupidity made him wander farther down the trail than was safe.*

cunning (adj.) sly, clever at deceit *His cunning plan had us in the girl's dorm in no time.*

imperative 1. (adj.) super important and necessary It *is imperative that you are there on time, for we cannot start without you.*

arbitrary (adj.) based on things or ideas that appear random *His choice of dates appears arbitrary – there is no rhyme or reason to it.*

Difficulties

onerous (adj.) hard to do, hard to make *The payments on the car became onerous, it was just too much for my monthly budget, and I had to sell it.*

perfunctory (adj.) without effort, enthusiasm or interest *It was strange how perfunctory the sports announcer's remarks were with the exciting events occurring on the field.*

harrowing (adj.) distressing, frightening *The few hours we spend lost in the woods was a harrowing experience.*

inextricable (adj.) tangled or entangled severely *The inextricable situation baffled everyone, no one could find a solution.*

tremulous (adj.) scared, nervous *I was a bit tremulous walking down the dark path alone at night.*

atypical (adj.) unusual or unexpected *Ralph was always talking, so his quiet behavior tonight was atypical.*

nebulous (adj.) unclear; vaguely described *The movie was so confusing, who was the good guy and who was the bad guy was nebulous.*

ostracism (n.) exclusion from a group or club *Charlie was ostracized from the diet club for bringing an ice cream cake to the meeting.*

notorious (adj.) famous in a negative way, infamous *The professor was notorious for arriving late to class.*

defile (v.) to make dirty, impure, to ruin *The atmosphere in the quiet room was defiled by the horrible music blasting from next door.*

reprehensible (adj.) terrible, deserving insult and scorn *Breaking up with your girlfriend on Valentine's Day is reprehensible.*

flout (v.) to disregard, disobey or openly ignore *He flouted the restaurant's dress code and was promptly escorted out.* It was inappropriate to wear a FLOUTered dress to the ball game.

iniquity (n.) sinful, wicked, unfair *My girlfriend would not forgive my iniquitous behavior and dumped me.*

recalcitrant (adj.) defiant, sticking to one's guns, unyeilding *The recalcitrant guard refused entry to the king because of his earlier orders.*

imperious (adj.) commanding, domineering, overbearing *His imperious nature made me dislike him immediately.* The IMPERIOUS emperor from Star Wars was commanding and mean.

restive (adj.) stubborn, impatient, resistant or argumentative *The seasoned comedian took apart the restive heckler.* I want to be RESTIVE! No you don't! YES I DO. NO YOU DON'T!

quagmire (n.) a tough or overly complicated situation *Many feel the Vietnam War was a true quagmire for the American military.* Glen Quagmire from "Family Guy" is always in difficult situations.

disaffected (adj.) rebellious, resentful of authority *Arty was a bad kid – picking on other kids and disaffected all the time.* DIS AFFECTED his grades.

Distribution

abdicate – (verb) to give up a position of power or rule *The king abdicated his throne to marry the commoner.*

retract (v.) to take back, withdraw *He retracted his statement about his opponent when it turned out it was completely false.*

inundate (v.) to overload with *Since publishing Professor Dave's Owner's Manual for the SAT and ACT essays, I have been inundated with requests to grade essays.*

procure (v.) to get *I saved up enough money to procure a new smartphone.*

abort (v.) to give up on or cancel *The men decided to abort the mission when one of them became ill.*

congregation (n.) a gathering of people, usually for religious services *The rabbi told a funny story to the congregation.*

abscond (v) to hide or sneak away *I absconded with an extra piece of grandma's pie.*

convene (v.) to call a group together *The mayor convened his top advisors.*

revoke (v.) to take back, cancel *After seven speeding tickets, his license was revoked.*

excavate (v.) to remove from the ground via digging *The site was fully excavated when dinosaur remains were found nearby.*

allocate (v.) to distribute, give out, set aside *I allocated the candy at the party the best I could, but I knew the kids would be unhappy anyway.*

attain (v.) to achieve, to get *He attained the position of CEO after years of hard work.*

bequeath (v.) to give to after death *My television was bequeathed to me by my late uncle.*

confluence (n.) a gathering together of people or ideas *The confluence of weather, people, and music made for a perfect night. Remember this word with the famous card game – "Magic – The Confluence."*

defer (v.) to postpone something; to yield to another's wisdom *He deferred to her expertise when choosing a cell phone.*

coronation (n.) the act of crowning, making of royalty *His coronation took place over a long weekend with terrific weather.*

disseminate (v.) to spread widely, to give out to many *He disseminated his thesis to everyone in the senior class.*

Existence

integral (adj.) required for completeness *Jason is an integral part of our team. Without him, we are no good.*

circumscribed (adj.) marked off, bounded, delineated *The swimming area of the lake was clearly circumscribed by ropes in the water.*

nomadic (adj.) wandering from place to place, not indigenous *The nomadic musician never stayed in one city for long; he travelled from place to place seeking work.*

antediluvian (adj.) ancient *The antediluvian ruins of Greece are fascinating.*

insular (adj.) of an island; separate and narrow-minded, provincial *Those in top-secret agencies tend to be insular, not interacting with us "regular people."*

neophyte (n.) newbie; one who is young or inexperienced *A neophyte in the corporate world, Jessie had trouble getting his ideas listened to.*

extant (adj.) existing still *The threat of war is always extant in a great nation.*

obsolete (adj.) no longer in use, out of date *DVD and CD players and recorders have made VHS machines practically obsolete.*

nominal (adj.) minor, small, insignificant *Entrance to the museum required a nominal fee which we happily paid.*

disavow (v.) to deny knowledge of or responsibility for *Any fan of "Mission Impossible" knows the word disavow: "Should you be caught, we will disavow any knowledge of your existence…"*

gourmand (n.) one who especially enjoys eating and drinking *Once a fussy eater, Lexis has become quite the gourmand in recent years.*

aggregate 1. (n.) the sum of or total *The three teams together represent an aggregate much greater than any one of them.* 2. (v.) to gather into a group *The sergeant aggregated as many men as he could and led the charge.*

dirge (n.) a sad song, especially for a funeral *The dirge played at the funeral will stick in my memory forever.*

anarchy (n.) lack of government or order *Anarchy reigned after the collapse of the democratic government in power.*

ardor (n.) vigor, energy, enthusiasm *The team shouted as it skated onto the ice – showing its ardor for all to observe.*

clandestine (adj.) secret, hidden *He kept a clandestine word list behind his watch, but still did not pass the vocabulary test.*

Explanations

esoteric (adj.) understood by only a select few *Professor Dave's Owner's Manual for the SAT is most certainly NOT esoteric – anyone can benefit from reading it.*

elucidate (v.) to clarify or explain *After the difficult lecture, I asked my roommate, who is expert in the subject, to elucidate.* After LUCYSDATE I asked her to explain everything.

officious (adj.) offering services when they are neither wanted nor needed *Never be officious – it's better to answer only when asked.*

obfuscate (v.) to make incomprehensible or extremely confusing *The professor's assignment was surely designed to obfuscate the students.*

oration (n.) a speech or message delivered formally *The heckler interrupted the president's oration and was quickly removed from the room.*

incarnate (adj.) the flesh version of – to make into human flesh *The small child was so evil natured we called him the "devil incarnate."* Be human – get in the CAR,NATE."

figurative (adj.) symbolic or suggestive, metaphorical *He spoke in a figurative manner, never directly describing anything, only hinting at it.* The FIGURATIVE statue was a symbol.

quaint (adj.) charmingly old-fashioned, cute *The quaint cottages along the shore were charming and homey.*

equivocal (adj.) ambiguous, uncertain, undecided *His answer was so equivocal I had no idea after hearing it if he was going with us or not.*

ostensible (adj.) seemingly, apparently *Sheryl's reason for taking the train was ostensibly that it was faster than flying, but she really just didn't like airplanes.*

agriculture (n.) farming *In an agriculture based society, weather is a huge factor on the economy.*

manifold (adj.) diverse, different, varied *The Harry Potter books offer manifold story lines.*

lurid (adj.) shocking, sensational *The lurid descriptions of the lover's antics was too much for the young adult book, and they had to be edited out.*

bereft (adj.) without (usually followed by "of") *He was bereft of money after his spending spree.*

culmination (n.) the ending toward which something moves *The vicious argument culminated in their agreement never to speak to one another again.*

chronological (adj.) in time order *Putting all of my high school essays in chronological order really showed me how I have improved as a writer.*

inclination (n.) a tendency towards *His inclination to surf in waves too big for him will cost him someday!*

enfranchise (v.) to give voting power to *The 19th amendment of the United States Constitution enfranchised women.*

encore (n.) a continuation of a performance, an extra performance *The concert was great since the band did encore after encore.*

acoustics (n.) the quality of sound in a room *The acoustics of the old church were so good it was the perfect place to hold our concert.*

inane (adj.) ridiculous *His inane comments made us laugh for hours.*

pliable (adj.) flexible, bendable *Rudders on boats are pliable so as not to break if pulled too swiftly.*

comprehensive (adj.) including everything, covering all *I have a comprehensive exam next week – it covers everything we have studied up to this point.*

Generosity and Concern

altruistic (adj.) Giving or generous with time or money *Her altruistic ways had others call her a true philanthropist.* AL, its TRUE, and gives his money away.

lavish 1. (adj.) without limits, extreme *My new book was so well received the critics showered me with lavish praise.* 2. (v.) to give without limits *Because the book was so well received, the critics lavished me with praise.*

benevolent (adj.) goodness, kindness *His benevolent gift of a playground to the school will be remembered by children in this town for a long time.* My friend BENE (Benny) is very kind.

magnanimous (adj.) generous, kind, giving *The magnanimous usher took pity on us and moved other people so we could sit together.* Volcanoes can laughably be called MAGNAnimous…they are so giving with their lava!

philanthropic (adj.) charitable, giving (especially with money) *Warren Buffet is known as philanthropic; the billionaire constantly gives huge amounts of money to charity.*

largess (n.) the generous giving of grand gifts *Giving a new boat as a prize was an example of the largess characteristic of the millionaire.* I want the LARGESS present under the tree!

munificence (n.) generosity in giving or treatment *Once the business went viral, the owner gave everyone huge bonuses, following through on the munificence he had promised.*

propriety (n.) the quality of behaving properly, decently, with good manners and behavior *I say we should ignore propriety when it comes to mini-skirts.*

cultivate (v.) to nurture, improve, refine or grow *He cultivated his love of fiction with the J. D. Robb "Death" collection.*

prudence (n.) cautious, smart thinking, conservative action *Practicing great prudence, my sister Prudence saved a lot of money over the summer.*

didactic 1. (adj.) intended to *His didactic manner made him very popular with his friends — he was always teaching them something cool.* 2. (adj.) overly moralistic *His didactic ways were sometimes interpreted as "preachy".*

allay (v.) to soothe, ease, make better *The woman tried to allay her daughter's fears during the thunderstorm.*

Happy and Joyful

euphoric (adj.) extremely happy, thrilled *I was euphoric when I found out I was accepted to Harvard.*

rapport (n.) mutual understanding, getting along with harmoniously *When they met, there was an instant rapport.*

elated (adj.) overjoyed, thrilled, super happy *My friend Elaine is always elated, for she is the happiest person I know.*

kudos (n.) praise for an achievement or accomplishment *Kudos to Steven for his superb SAT score.*

cordial (adj.) warm, affectionate, sweet (in attitude) *Her cordial manner makes her a pleasure to be around.*

exult (v.) to rejoice, celebrate *Upon receiving the award, I exulted by dancing around in a circle.*

ecstatic (adj.) intensely happy *The man was ecstatic when he learned his wife was carrying twins.*

placid (adj.) calm, peaceful, tranquil *The lake was so placid in the morning it looked like a sheet of glass.* Lake PLACID is where they held the most peaceful Olympics.

sanguine (adj.) optimistic, cheerful *Even the loss of her favorite dog could not quell Misty's sanguine spirits.*

palatable (adj.) tasty, pleasant *The meal looked weird, but it tasted quite palatable.*

sensual (adj.) involving sensory gratification, usually sexually related *Her sensual smile was hard to resist.*

hedonism (n.) believing pleasure should be the most important thing in life *Hedonistic vacations sell very well to the twenty to thirty year old crowd.*

tranquil (adj.) peaceful *My favorite time of day is the tranquil few moments just before the sun comes up; the world seems to be on "pause."*

enamor (v.) to feel love towards (usually used with "of" or "to") *He was enamored of fishing and tried to go whenever he could.*

jubilant (adj.) joyful, happy *They were such a great couple that everyone was jubilant when they finally were married.*

convivial (adj.) celebratory, usually featuring feasting, drinking, merriment *The convivial atmosphere at their party was second to none, for I had a great time.*

consonant (adj.) in harmony, sounds good *The consonant orchestra was perfect.*

I Am, Therefore, I Am

engender (v.) to create or generate (as in a feeling) *The 1980 Olympic Hockey Team engendered patriotism throughout the United States.*

arboreal (adj.) having to do with or related to trees *Koala bears are arboreal creatures, they live most of their lives atop Eucalyptus trees.*

cognizant (adj.) aware of, mindful *She was cognizant of the fact that men can not always be trusted.*

ascribe (v.) to assign, attribute to *Many ascribe the fortune cookie's invention to the Chinese, but it was actually an American invention.*

nascent (adj.) in the middle of being born or being generated *The nascent policy was quickly rumored throughout the company before it had even been completed.*

audible (adj.) able to be heard *Their argument was audible through the paper-thin walls.*

circuitous (adj.) roundabout, not direct *Looking to make a few extra bucks, the taxi driver took a circuitous route to the hotel.*

empirical 1. (adj.) observed or experienced *My empirical knowledge of smoothies comes from my many kitchen experiments.* I observed the EMPERORicals new clothes!

aerial (adj.) related to the air or sky *The huge group of hot air balloons was an amazing aerial spectacle.* The AERIAL antennae gets signals through the air.

transient (adj.) brief, momentary *Most of the traffic in the small town was transient; very few people stayed as most were just passing through on their way elsewhere.*

soluble (adj.) able to dissolve *No matter how many times it is tried, oil is not soluble in water.*

vicissitude (n.) something that occurs by chance *Getting the winning ticket was a pure example of vicissitude.*

fastidious (adj.) extremely careful, demanding, having high and often unattainable standards *I am so fastidious that nothing ever seems finished to my satisfaction.*

Improve Your Situation

exculpate (v.) to free from guilt or blame *When he found his wallet, he exculpated his friend who he had accused of stealing it.*

mollify (v.) to soften in temper, make feel better *Even the manager could not mollify the angry customer.* My friend MOLLI always calms everyone down – she's a peacemaker.

absolution (n.) release from guilt, sin or blame *Upon investigation, I was absolved of having stolen the extra piece of pie.*

expiate (v.) to make up for , atone *To expiate for running over her flowers, I bought her a whole pallet of beautiful begonias.*

mitigate (v.) to make less violent, to make better, to relieve *A cold compress was the only thing that could mitigate my bad headache.*

accentuate (v.) to highlight or bring attention to *Her lovely coat accentuated her slim figure.*

foster (v.) to promote, take care of, encourage *To foster better health, schools are removing sugary snacks from their cafeterias.* Bananas FOSTER is a helpful food.

atone (v.) to repent, make inner peace with, to act to obtain forgiveness *It is easier not to make mistakes than to try and atone them later.* Inner peace occurs when one is AT-ONE with one's self.

lucid (adj.) clear, easily understood *The essay was so lucid I understood it all in one quick read.*

ameliorate (v.) to make better *He ameliorated his situation by getting a new job.* Amelia made it better for women flyers.

console (v.) to comfort and sooth *I was unable to console him after his best friend moved across the country.*

buttress 1. (v.) to support, hold up *We buttressed the table with rocks and wood.*

boon (n.) gift, blessing, positive addition *His new royalty arrangement was a boon to his savings.*

conciliatory (adj.) friendly, agreeable, nice *He spoke in such a conciliatory way everyone felt at ease.*

amenable (adj.) willing, going along with, cooperative *Dad was amenable to driving us to 7-11, he likes slurpees too.*

Holy Holy

consecrate (v.) to dedicate something to a holy purpose, to make holy *The land was consecrated by the church after the miracle that occurred there.*

knell (n.) dark, foreboding sound, usually made by a bell, sometimes indicating death *The death knell of the church bells cast a gloomy air over the town.*

orthodox (adj.) conventional, standard *The orthodox ways of saving money still work wonderfully in this modern world: Consistency, conscientiousness, care.*

talisman (n.) lucky charm; item designed to protect one from supernatural forces *He carried an ancient Native American talisman for protection from evil clouds.*

hallowed (adj.) held in special regard; revered, holy *Try to visit the hallowed gallery of the Notre Dame cathedral if you ever travel to France.*

exogamy (n.) marriage outside of one's specific group or tribe *When the Native American woman married the Chinese man, the exogamy was looked upon with wonder and intrigue.*

maxim (n.) a common position expressing a standard of conduct *The team's maxims are clearly posted on the locker room wall.*

paragon (n.) perfect or excellent example *She was, quite simply, the paragon of beauty.*

dogmatic (adj.) aggressively and strongly certain about unproved principles and ideas *His dogmatic attitude pissed everyone off; even his dog.*

anachronistic (adj.) out of correct chronological order or not in the right time period *In the classic film Ben Hur, several Roman soldiers are seen wearing digital watches – a big anachronistic error.*

NOTES

I'm Better Than You Are (or at least I think so)

potentate (n.) one with great power, a ruler *The potentate's new policies were well received by the populace.*

contempt (n.) disrespect, thinking lower of something or someone *His contempt for the teacher was obvious, and it cost him a good grade.*

egotist (n.) someone who thinks he or she is better than everyone else *He was such an egotist no one would speak to him.*

audacious (adj.) excessively bold, ballsy *His audacious manner shocked the interviewer – telling him he was to be the owner of the company in a few short years.*

pretentious (adj.) acting better than one really is; false self-aggradation *Her boyfriend, who was unemployed, was very pretentious – giving everyone career advice.*

canny (adj.) shrewd, careful, planning in advance *The canny jockey waited until the perfect moment to rush his mount forward.*

disdain (v.) to scorn, hold in low esteem, insult *The new singers were disdained by the veterans of the group even though they showed great talent.*

complacency (n.) self-satisfied, ignorant of danger *His complacency preparing for the SAT led to his poor score.*

haughty (adj.) boastful, overly proud *Many actors are known for being haughty with the press.* Being haughty is like being proud of being naughty.

narcissistic (adj.) in love with oneself, egotistic *Narcissa Malfoy was in love with herself, she was very narcissistic.*

ostentatious (adj.) excessively showy, glitzy *The tour showed us most of the ostentatious holdings of the royal family, but little of its history.*

diligent (adj.) showing care in one's work, paying careful attention *The diligent scientist checked everything twice.*

alacrity (n.) skill, enthusiasm, speed *He mowed the lawn with alacrity, knowing we would leave for the ballpark when he was finished.*

wily (adj.) crafty, sly *The wily criminal dressed in black so as not to be seen.*

bourgeois (n.) a middle-class person *His attitude was quite bourgeois – he wanted a simple, comfortable existence.*

Items of Interest

conduit (n.) a connector – usually a pipe or wire *The electricity passed through the conduit – it was conducted across the wire.*

delegate (v.) to give out jobs; to give responsibility to others under your command *Before the party, mom delegated chores to each of us. She made us DELEGATES.*

contemporaneous (adj.) existing during the same time, contemporaries *The great artist Benini's work was contemporaneous with that of Michelangelo.*

coup 1. (n.) a clever and unexpected act *Charles pulled quite a coup getting the professor to postpone the test by spilling tea on his desk.* 2. (n.) the overthrow of a government and assumption of authority *The coup in Cuba in the 1940's has effects that are still felt today.*

kindle (v.) to light (as in a fire); to start, be a catalyst *The girls poem kindled his interest in writing poetry of his own.*

antecedent (n.) something that came before *The antecedents of the U.S. Constitution harken all the way back to the Magna Carta.*

seminal (adj.) original, important, groundbreaking *Some of Einstein's work was seminal in the field of nuclear physics.*

tome (n.) a large book, usually of knowledge *What I don't know about women would fill a tome.*

epistolary (adj.) relating to letter writing or letters *A pen pal and I have kept up an epistolary relationship for over twenty years.* When I need to mail a letter I go to the EPISTOLARY office.

ironic (adj.) bizarre in outcome, opposite of expected happening *The fire marshal gave us the ironic news – the smoke detector's wiring had shorted out causing the fire.*

anthology (n.) a selected collection of an artist's work *Believe it or not, the Beatles anthology only encompasses nine hours of music.*

caucus (n.) a meeting for like-minded people with a common goal *The union members held a caucus to discuss what they would request in the new contract.*

aberration – (noun) something out of the ordinary, unexpected *The short basketball player was an aberration.* It was so cold in Hawaii it was an aBURRRRation

maelstrom (n.) a powerful whirlpool which rapidly sucks things in *When you drain the tub, you create a miniature maelstrom by the drain.*

injunction (n.) an order of official warning from an authority *The shaving cream abuse at Halloween prompted the town council to adopt an injunction against anyone under the age of 18 buying shaving cream.*

turbulence (n.) difficult times, confusing times, shakiness in an aircraft *The turbulence of the early 1960's led to the TURBANlence of the 2000's.*

combustion (n.) the act or process of burning *The combination of air and heat resulted in combustion of the wood.*

commensurate (adj.) the same size or amount as *The money in the project was commensurate with the experience of the participants.*

balk (v.) to stop or block suddenly, verbally *Lexie balked at the idea of eating two gallons of ice cream in one night.*

arable (adj.) farmable – able to be used for agriculture *The land north of the snow line is rarely arable.*

contusion – (noun) a bruise or injury *He suffered many contusions in the accident.* With so many bruises, there was confusion over his CONTUSION

semaphore (n.) a visual signal or sign *The lifeguards worked out a system of semaphores to communicate along the large beach.*

demarcation (n.) the indication of or marking of boundaries or categories *The demarcation of the church has changed over the centuries.*

buffet 1. (v.) to strike with force repeatedly *The strong wind buffeted the windows.* 2. (n.) an arrangement of food set out on a table *My friend joked that "buffet" is a French word that means "Get up and get it yourself."*

dialect (n.) variation in language usually associated with a geographic location *A different dialect of Italian is spoken in Sicily than is spoken on mainland Italy.*

edict (n.) an order, rule, or decree *My instructor's edicts include stretching, jogging, and weight training.*

innuendo (n.) subtle hint *He made several innuendos about the behavior of his friend.*

liability 1. (n.) a legal responsibility, usually monetary *My loan from my parents is a huge liability.* **2.** (n.) a handicap, burden, or hardship *The weak fielder was a liability for the otherwise stalwart team.*

choreography (n.) arrangement of dances or dance steps *The musical featured some wonderful choreography – the dancers were fabulous.*

paradox (n.) an unsolvable circular puzzle, something that seems impossible yet is true *The president struggled with the paradox that the best way to obtain peace is to increase defense spending.*

zenith (n.) the highest point, very top *The band Tommy Tutone reached the zenith of its career with the hit "867-5309/Jenny."* A ZENITH TV is the very top brand.

myriad (adj.) a very great number of *The buffet featured myriad food choices.* My friend MYRI can ADD huge numbers of things in her head.

NOTES

Make It Better

contrite (adj.) seeking forgiveness, genuinely sorry *The puppy had such a contrite look on his face it was impossible to be mad at him for knocking over the garbage.*

alleviate (v.) to relieve, make easier or more bearable *The aspirin alleviated the pain of her headache.*

resolve 1. (v.) to find a solution *With some creative math, he resolved the difference between his bank balance and his checkbook's balance.* 2. (v.) to decide firmly *The twins resolved to dress differently from that day forward.*

efficacious (adj.) effective *His technique for studying vocabulary proved efficacious; we could remember all the words we had learned by associating things with them.*

placate (v.) to make less angry, cool-off someone *My father could not be placated after the waiter spilled his soup on him and refused to bring him another bowl.*

replete (adj.) full of, abundant with *My father's boat is replete with everything the fisherman might need.*

auspicious (adj.) favorable, meaning good things are coming *His practice sessions were auspicious; he went into the match supremely confident.*

satiate (v.) to satisfy completely or a bit too much *The 64oz. drink satiated my thirst.*

compunction (n.) distress caused by guilt *She felt compunction because of how she spoke to him on the phone.*

repentant (adj.) sorry, sadness over actions *The repentant scholar apologized for the blatant error in the text.*

palliate (v.) to reduce the severity of, make better or tolerable *When all hope of cure is lost, sometimes people are placed in palliative care facilities to make their last days more pleasant.*

reconcile 1. (v.) to return to peace *A well-timed case of beer helped the feuding neighbors reconcile.* 2. (v.) to make agree with existing conditions *Reconciling his philosophy was easy once one explored the reasoning behind it.*

amenity (n.) an item that increases comfort or luxury *I truly enjoy the amenities of the beach house when we go on vacation.*

emollient (adj.) soothing *I need an emollient balm to make my sunburn feel better.*

panacea (n.) cure-all *Wouldn't it be great if there were a panacea in pill form? No one would ever be sick again.*

pacify (v.) to calm down another or a situation *He was able to pacify the angry baby by playing with her – he was a true pacifier.*

analgesic (n.) pain reducer *Aspirin is the most popular analgesic in the world.*

appease (v.) to calm down, to satisfy *To appease the customer, the manager gave her a coupon redeemable for a free replacement.*

mediate (v.) to resolve a conflict as a third party *He mediated the fight between his parents.*

arbitration (n.) the process of resolving a dispute *When the team and its star player could not agree on a contract, it went to arbitration.*

quell (v.) to control a potentially bad or dangerous situation *He quelled the riot by buying everyone a drink. "Quell with quaff!" he said.*

assuage (v.) to ease, make better, make calmer *She assuaged my fears of flying so effectively I actually enjoyed the flight.*

benign (adj.) mild, harmless *His tumor was described as benign, much to his relief.*

streamline (v.) to reduce waste, to make more efficient *He streamlined his plan to save money.*

Make It Worse

debase (v.) to lower the quality of *When the candles were replaced with lights the mood of the room debased rapidly.*

wizened (adj.) dry, shrunken, wrinkled *His advanced years gave him a wizened look about him.*

exasperate (v.) to irritate, piss-off *The store owner's never ending description was exasperating. Just sell it to me, okay?*

confound (v.) to frustrate, confuse, mislead *The thief confounded police trying to follow him by laying a false trail. The cops "cantfound" him.*

wallow (v.) to feel sorry for oneself to the point of doing nothing *After their breakup, he wallowed in self-pity for weeks. It was very sad.*

atrophy (v.) to wither away, decay, shrink Her dramatic description of my house plants – atrophied – prompted me to pay more attention to them.

blight 1. (n.) a plague, disease, problem *The blight of 1812 killed over 20,000 people in the small city.* 2. (n.) something that takes away hope and positive thoughts *His blight was felt throughout the battalion, causing many problems.*

squander (v.) to waste *He squandered his winnings in one night, spending foolishly on ridiculous purchases.*

adversity (n.) hardship, tough times *Dealing with adversity can test the character of any person.*

convoluted (adj.) intricate, complicated, confusing *The young student offered such a convoluted story for his absence it was impossible to believe.*

morose (adj.) gloomy, sullen, depressed *After the breakup, Carly was morose for weeks.*

hamper (v.) to hold back, make more difficult He was hampered by the closed lid on the hamper – he could not toss his socks in from across the room.

truculent (adj.) mean, nasty, ready to fight *The truculent man was always getting into scuffles.* TRUCdrivers are always mean!

belligerent (adj.) always looking for a fight, warlike, nasty *Her belligerent attitude really pissed me off, for she was always looking for a fight.*

egregious (adj.) terrible, awful *Dropping water balloons on unsuspecting people is egregious behavior.*

forlorn (adj.) lonely, abandoned *When we broke up, I felt forlorn for a very long time.*

derail (v.) to take off a plan, to take off track *My plans were derailed to take the railroad throughout Europe when I ran out of money.*

exacerbate (v.) to make worse *The man exacerbated his problems with women's groups when he showed up for their meeting wearing a t-shirt that read, "Make Me A Sandwich"*

Mean and Nasty

disrepute (n.) being held in low regard or of poor opinion *The crew fell into disrepute when their pilfering was discovered.*

guile (n.) deceitful, cunning behavior *Since we was the king of guile, nothing the manager was accused of ever stuck.*

instigate (v.) to start trouble, cause unrest *The hockey player instigated the fight by putting his stick under the skate of his opponent.* Starting a fight in hockey is an INSTIGATE into the penalty box.

vindictive (adj.) vengeful; seeking revenge *Staying in the parking spot just to keep it from the nasty driver was a vindictive move.* My friend VIN is always seeking revenge.

insidious (adj.) appearing nice or good but imperceptibly harmful, seductive *His insidious use of laxatives in the otherwise fantastic brownies caused a huge problem for me later.*

contravene (v.) to contradict, oppose, violate, go against *On our trip, we contravened the hotel's rule about the number of people allowed in a room.*

incorrigible (adj.) can't be fixed, can't be corrected, innately bad or misbehaving *The youth was determined to be incorrigible and assigned to a correction facility by the judge.*

callous (adj.) cold, unfeeling, immune to the suffering of others *The criminal callously showed no remorse at his trial, which cost him a longer sentence.*

sanctimonious (adj.) giving a false appearance of being proper or pious *The sanctimonious councilor was fired after he screamed at people to quit drinking and then was found drunk in a bar.*

proscribe (v.) to condemn or make illegal *The railroad proscribed drinking alcoholic beverages on the train.* If you want to make something illegal, let a PRO SCRIBE it for you.

hegemony (n.) domination and control over others *The Roman Empire found it difficult to maintain its hegemony over its ever growing dominion.*

reprobate (adj.) evil, unprincipled, malicious *The reprobate crook showed no remorse in court, and the judge gave him a stiff sentence.* The repeat offender had no chance to go back on probation…he was reprobate.

mawkish (adj.) overly sentimental to the point of sickness *The poet's musings were so mawkish, I had to leave the room before I got ill.* MAWWWWWW….stop crying.

arrogate (v.) to seize without due process or justification *The arrogant dictator arrogated the right to assign punishments no longer allowing a jury to decide.*

wrath (n.) extreme anger, desire for revenge *The defendant incurred the wrath of the judge by burping while on the stand.*

ruse (n.) a clever trick *Patrick devised a clever ruse to sneak the car out of the garage without notice.*

turpitude (n.) moral corruption, evil *Known for his kind ways, he secretly practiced turpitude with people in private which was completely the opposite of what one would expect.*

inquisitor (n.) one who inquires, usually in a forceful or hostile manner *The inquisitor tortured the suspects until he was convinced of their innocence or guilt.*

pilfer (v.) to steal a small amount from a larger stock *We almost didn't catch the fact that he was pilfering a few coins a day from the register.*

enmity (n.) ill will, hatred, hostility *(Doug and Joseph have clearly not forgiven each other, because the enmity between them is obvious to anyone in their presence.)*

disparage (v.) to criticize verbally *The car salesman disparaged his competition's offerings, calling them "tin boxes of doom."*

insolent (adj.) rude, arrogant, nasty *Telling the teacher she was ugly was a very insolent thing to say.*

noxious (adj.) harmful, toxic *Noxious chemicals in the water are very dangerous.*

indignation (n.) feeling slighted by unfairness, offended *His indignation over his lack of promotion was deep and genuine.*

assail (v.) to attack *She assailed him when she found out he was cheating on her.*

bane (n.) a burden, hardship, or enemy *Calculus is the bane of my academic existence.*

berate (v.) to scream at or scold *The author berated his editor when he found several errors in the manuscript.*

clamor 1. (n.) a loud noise *The trucks going by on the highway made such a clamor we checked out of the hotel early.* 2. (v.) to insist loudly *After the incredibly music, the crowd clamored for an encore.*

ignominious (adj.) embarrassing to the extreme, humiliating *He was ignominiously kicked out of the Android club for owning an iPhone.*

malicious (adj.) evil, bad *The malicious character in the brilliant film, "Inception" is named "Mal" because she's a bad influence.*

NOTES

Money Matters

indigent (adj.) very poor, broke (money) *After the collapse of his life – his marriage, job, and car all gone – he lived in an indigent way for years.*

frugal (adj.) careful and thrifty with money *Mary's frugal ways always result in her buying store brands rather than the more expensive name brands.*

mercenary (adj.) thinking only of money-making, greedy *The mercenaries were hired guns – but they ran when the fighting got nasty.*

solvent (adj.) able to pay debts and liabilities *When Rick's birthday money arrived, he was suddenly solvent.*

embezzle (v.) to steal money by falsifying accounts *The manager was caught embezzling from the Christmas Fund.*

opulent (adj.) displaying wealth in an obvious way *The lieutenant's quarters were incredibly opulent compared to the soldiers' barracks.*

collateral 1. (adj.) secondary *The collateral damage from the flood was worse than the flood itself.* 2. (n.) security for a debt *He left his expensive watch as collateral for the loan.*

thrifty (adj.) very careful with money, spending little *His parents taught him to be thrifty – so when he opened a store that sold items cheaply, he called it "The Thrifty Shop."*

miserly (adj.) very tight with money to the point of cheapness *His miserly ways earned him a reputation for being cheap.*

prodigal (adj.) wasteful, excessively lavish *The prodigal son – the one who never had enough money is his pocket – asked his father for a loan for the fortieth time.*

penurious (adj.) stingy, cheap (attitude) *He was so penurious he refused to split the cost of the popcorn with us even though he ate most of it.*

avarice (n.) tremendous greed *Although many call him avaricious, Steve Jobs was simply a mean guy.*

austere (adj.) simple, plain, poor *The austere decor of the inn was very disappointing.*

parsimony (n.) stinginess, cheapness *With his typical parsimony, he left a small tip for the hard-working waitress. He doesn't like to part-with-his-money.*

exorbitant (adj.) excessive (usually used to refer to a price or cost) *The exorbitant number given my father to repair his truck turned him a dark shade of red.*

affluent (adj.) wealthy *He was quite affluent; he owned several cars, a beautiful gold watch, and a small island off the coast of Maine.*

destitute (adj.) extremely poor (financially) *The tsunami left many coastal residents destitute.*

consummate (v.) to complete a deal; to complete a marriage ceremony through sexual intercourse *The couple consummated their deal in the fancy bathroom.*

remuneration (n.) pay; earnings *His remuneration for the week was impressive; he earned several hundred dollars more than his friend did.*

Nasty Talk

defamatory (adj.) harmful toward one's reputation *The defamatory remarks made by the candidate were well-received by the crowd. He tried to DEFAME him—remove his fame— deFAMatory.*

bigot (n.) person who exhibits racisim or prejudice *When he spoke of his employees, he showed what a bigot he was – only women could do the kitchen tasks.*

inarticulate (adj.) incapable of expressing oneself using speech *The inarticulate professor left his students wondering what the heck he was talking about on a daily basis.*

incendiary 1. (n.) one who causes trouble *They are looking for the incendiary that screamed "FIRE" in the crowded theatre.* 2. (adj.) inflammatory, causing burning *The incendiary device used to light the barbeque was simple – a match.*

cantankerous (adj.) cranky, nasty, mean *The cantankerous old man was always screaming at kids in the street.*

abase (verb) to embarrass or degrade *The abased politician resigned rather than be removed from office.* At the baseball field, I ran around *abase* naked – man, was I embarrassed!

strident (adj.) harsh, loud, nasty *The strident commands of the ship's captain could be heard over the crashing waves.*

pugnacious (adj.) argumentative, combative *Rich is slow pugnacious I'm afraid he might bite!* That little PUG is nasty and combative.

denounce (v.) to criticize publicly *The man denounced his opponent as a cheater.*

impute (v.) to attach blame, accuse *The guard imputed the cleaner for stealing supplies.*

obstreperous (adj.) noisy, unruly, misbehaving *His obstreperous behavior at the museum caused the docent to call security and have him removed.*

inimical (adj.) hostile, enemy-like *Growing up with inimical neighbors can be difficult.*

abject (adj.) very bad, pitiful *After she fell into a puddle, Debbie was abject and miserable.* It is pitiful to ABJECT or OBJECT

flagrant (adj.) offensive or wrong, in an obvious or severe way *The tripping of the other player was a flagrant violation of the rules.*

illicit (adj.) forbidden, not allowed *The pictures were illicit and therefore promptly removed from the website.*

coerce (v.) to have something done by force or threat *The man's confession did not hold up in court since it was shown he was coerced into signing it.*

rancor (n.) bitter resentment *It was obvious the boxers hated each other by the rancor clearly visible in their eyes.*

eschew (v.) to avoid or shun contact with *My sister shuns the movies after a bad experience one evening last year.*

stupefy (v.) to astonish, utterly confuse *He stupefied us with his inane explanation – we had no idea what he was talking about.*

duress (n.) difficulty, threat *Under duress for over an hour, the soldiers finally returned fire.* For me, a guy, wearing a DURESS would be a problem.

noisome (adj.) stinky, offensive, especially to the sense of smell *In the small room, her overabundance of perfume was noisome.*

licentious (adj.) having a lack of moral or legal restraints *The former governor of New York turned out to have led a licentious existence outside of the office.* Do you need a LICENTIOS to act this way?

disgruntled (adj.) unhappy with the state of things *The disgruntled employee had a shouting match with his manager in the parking lot.*

presumptuous (adj.) rude or disrespectfully bold *My friend found it presumptuous that he tried to kiss her on the first date.*

connive (v.) plotting, scheming *He connived to steal my taco when I wasn't looking.*

scathing (adj.) critical and very hurtful *His scathing accusations had the entire courtroom breathless.*

grievous (adj.) injurious, harmful or hurtful in a large or serious manner *The politician made a grievous error which essentially ended his bid for office.*

bilk (v.) to cheat or defraud *Bernie Madoff bilked his clients out of billions of dollars.*

putrid (adj.) rotten, foul, stinky *Whatever was on the plate we left on the table all summer has turned putrid.*

umbrage (n.) resentment, offense, insult *I took umbrage when the man called me a coward.* Dolores UMBRAGE from Harry Potter was always insulting Harry.

refute (v.) to prove incorrect *Marco refuted the argument by showing how it was not possible.*

NOTES

Nice

affable (adj.) friendly, amiable   *Geo is affable and good-natured, so people enjoy being around him.*

empathy (n.) feeling what another is feeling as if it were one's own   *Twins have been known to exhibit intense empathy for one another.*

resplendent (adj.) glowing, looking radiant, looking great   *She was resplendent in her black dress.*

commendation (n.) notice of approval   *Jane received a commendation at work for saving the company lots of money on the new project.*

lenient (adj.) tolerant, easy-going when responding to something   *The other police officer thought he was too lenient letting the speeder go with just a warning.*

clemency (n.) mercy   *The judge granted clemency on the young offender, shortening his sentence.*

fortuitous (adj.) lucky or fortunate   *His fortuitous nature never ceases to amaze me, for I simply cannot beat him at cards. Perhaps it's his long sleeves…*

judicious (adj.) exercising or having sound judgment   *Selling the house while the market was high was a very judicious decision.*

accolade (n.) high praise   *His great performance earned him many critical accolades.*

accommodating (adj.) helpful, polite, cooperative   *The hotel clerk was so accommodating we enjoyed many things we never would have known about otherwise.*

deferential (adj.) respect for another's authority   *His deferential attitude towards the professor went a long way to his selection as assistant.*

adulation (n.) praise   *His book received the adulation of his peers, they thought it was terrific.*

genial (adj.) kind, friendly, likeable   *I find my sister's husband very genial, he's a really nice guy.*

congenial (adj.) pleasantly agreeable, nice, friendly *Conny's congenial manner made her friends wherever she went.*

amicable (adj.) friendly, likeable *Your sister is so friendly she may be the most amicable person I know.*

winsome (adj.) charming, pleasant *Always winsome, Sarah is always smiling and friendly.*

approbation (n.) praise *The crowd approbated the returning soldiers.*

propitious (adj.) favorable, good *The propitious weather report promised a great day for boating.*

trenchant (adj.) easy to use, well made, effective *The instructions for cooking the bread were trenchant, we had no problems at all.*

affinity (n.) a feeling of closeness that usually comes on quickly *I felt an affinity for Steve the first time we met.*

amiable (adj.) friendly, nice AMI (read: Amy) *is so amiable, she gets along with everyone she meets.*

cherish (v.) to feel or show affection toward *My grandmother cherished her classical music collection.*

levity (adj.) funniness, lightness of heart, amusement *The Levy family are all funny, nice, and very friendly – they provide levity wherever they go.*

compliment (n.) an expression of approval; a nice thing to say about someone or something *You have nice eyes – that is a nice complIment (notice the I for nice I's)*

concord (n.) agreement *Once they decided to agree, concord was reached easily.*

Not Nice

demean (v.) to insult or put down, or cause to act of a lower station *It was demeaning for the former executive to serve coffee to the chairman, but that was his job now.*

calumny (n.) lying to spoil another's reputation *When the newspaper reported the illicit activities of the mayor, he screamed "Calumny!"*

appalling (adj.) inspiring shock, horror, disgust *His lack of concern for the litter of puppies was appalling.*

pilfer (v.) to steal in a sneaky manner *I knew someone was pilfering my Oreo cookies, I just didn't know who it was. When I find out – there will be a war.*

regurgitate 1. (v.) to vomit *The puppy regurgitated his dinner that he had eaten too quickly.* 2. (v.) to throw back exactly as issued *Vocabulary can be regurgitated if it is tested soon after it is learned. It is better, though, to learn it in a way that will help you remember it long term.*

pariah (n.) an outcast, someone "kicked out" of a group *After dropping the fly ball in the championship game, Tony felt like a pariah.*

depravity (n.) tastes that run to the dark, evil, wicked *His collection of movies can only be called depraved; he enjoys death and destruction.*

cloying (adj.) overly or annoyingly sweet *His cloying manner had me reaching for the barf bag immediately.*

acrimony (n.) bitterness, nastiness, disagreement *Acrimony developed between the brothers when they discovered they both loved the same woman.*

carp (v.) to annoy, to bug *His carping drove us crazy, so we kicked him out of the car.*

adverse (adj.) difficult, dangerous *The storm created such adverse conditions the only thing to do was stay inside and play Scrabble.*

affront (n.) an insult *The comment "her hair looked like a beehive" was taken as an affront.*

acrid (adj.) nasty, harsh, disgusting *The acrid smell in the apartment made it apparent it had not been cleaned since the last world war.*

despot (n.) one with absolute power who rules brutally *The despot made life in the small nation horrible.*

acerbic (adj) bitter or biting in flavor or taste *Her acerbic personality ensured she was alone most of the time.*

execrable (adj.) hateable, detestable *The painting was so execrable I could not believe someone actually bought it.*

bellicose (adj.) warlike, causing trouble, hostile *Her bellicose attitude ensured her friends would not talk to her for weeks.*

malediction (n.) curse *After the officer pulled away, my string of maledictions would have embarrassed a sailor.*

anguish (n.) extreme sadness, torment, torture (emotion) *Ron's anguish over leaving the group was apparent when he finally returned.*

beguile (v.) to trick, deceive, confuse *Many students find physics beguiling.*

antagonism (n.) hostility *Throughout the campaign, the candidates showed open antagonism toward one another.*

bias (n.) tendency, opinion based on previous ideas *His bias against rock music had him complaining about the concert before it even began.*

antipathy (n.) hatred or strong dislike *His antipathy towards his roommate's girlfriend was obvious.*

aspersion (n.) a curse or expression of ill-will *The arguing lawyers continued to cast aspersions on one another.*

chide (v.) to disapprove *Rose chided him for his bad haircut.*

animosity (n.) nastiness, hard feelings The dog obviously held animosity towards the man, he would not stop growling.

deleterious (adj.) harmful Computer viruses can be deleterious...so one should DELETE them as soon as possible.

NOTES

Not True!

dissemble – (v.) to hide, to fake *Not wanting to seem greedy or heartless, he dissembled his true intention of making money from the man's misfortune.* He lied about the DISSEMBLY – it was fake.

alias (n.) a false name or identity *Using an alias, he ordered items from his competition to see how they were doing business.*

fallacious (adj.) incorrect or misleading *His story about the dog was fallacious, we knew he had gone to the shelter, not a fancy puppy store.*

pretense (n.) appearance or action intended to fool *Wanting to go on a date, Carl borrowed his father's car under the pretense of needing to go to the library.*

hypocrisy (n.) saying one thing and doing the opposite *When the police chief was arrested for shoplifting, the hypocrisy was amazing.*

allege (v.) to accuse, usually without proof *The detective referred to the "alleged" theft of my car even though I was pretty damn sure it was missing.*

duplicity (n.) dishonesty, scam *His talent for duplicity was legendary – his simple manner made people believe whatever he said – but it was never true.*

apocryphal (adj.) fictitious, false, wrong, untrue *The story of him growing a third eye were apocryphal.*

counterfeit (adj.) fake; especially referring to money or goods *The counterfeit bills were so good even the bank had trouble picking them out of the pile.*

saccharine (adj.) overly sweet, as in manner or taste *Jennifer's saccharine manner was maddening sometimes.* To overly sweeten diet drinks, they use SACCHARINE.

mendacity (n.) lying. *His mendacity was appaling – he never told the truth. Girls, take note* men – in – da – city – LIE!

dubious (adj.) doubtful *His lack of skill on the court made his previous claims of being an all-star seem dubious.*

NOTES

Old Stuff

archaic (adj.) of or relating to an earlier period in time, not the current version *Joe insisted on using an archaic typewriter to prepare his thesis paper.* Taking an ARC to work would be an ARChaic means of travel.

antiquated (adj.) old, out of date *His antiquated coffeemaker was better at making mud than coffee.*

desiccated (adj.) dried up completely *The fruit was sitting for so long it was practically desiccated.*

derelict (adj.) abandoned, run-down, ruined *The derelict house at the end of the block was a real eyesore, so we requested the city tear it down.*

primeval (adj.) ancient, the first form of *His attitude was quite primeval – and would not bode well in the modern world.*

nostalgia (n.) remembering the past with fondness, sometimes inaccurately remembering it as better than it was *My grandfather would get nostalgic and tell us bread used to cost $.05 a loaf! He leaves out the part that he only earned $10 a week back then.*

venerable (adj.) deserving of respect because of age or achievement, of great worth because of age *The venerable furnishings in the house brought a huge amount of money at auction.*

dormant (adj.) sleeping, temporarily inactive *The volcano was dormant at the moment, but everyone in the town kept a watchful eye on it.*

NOTES

Opinions

exalt (v.) to glorify or praise *His performance on the SAT was exalted by his parents.*

intransigent (adj.) having extreme opinions and refusing to compromise *The intransigent child insisted on eating an entire half-gallon of ice cream until he was sick.*

compelling (adj.) demanding attention *The salesman's pitch was so compelling we bought it on the spot.*

quandary (n.) a perplexed, unresolvable state, confusing *My quandary was this: should I have chocolate or vanilla?*

abhor – (verb) to hate, detest *My sister abhors broccoli.* I hate prostitutes. I abWHORE them.

implicit (adj.) understood but not obvious, implied or strongly hinted at *He did not state outright that he wanted us to leave, but his body language was implicit, so we left.*

dogmatic - (adj.) aggressively opinionated about unproven things *His dogmatic ideas about his people angered those gathered.* My DOGMA thinks he knows everything.

accord (n.) an agreement *The union and management reached an accord after hours of debate.*

flabbergasted (adj.) shocked speechless; astounded; amazed *At the end of the mystery novel, I was flabbergasted at who the murderer turned out to be.*

aesthetic (adj.) artistic, referring to appreciation of beauty *His fine aesthetic sense made him a natural to decorate the hall for the dance.*

brazen (adj.) excessively bold, brash, sometimes rude *His brazen attempt to woo the girl angered her friends.*

extol (v.) to praise *The musician was extolled by his adoring fans.*

relish (v.) to enjoy *I relish relish with my hotdog; it's my favorite hot dog topping.*

antithesis (n.) total opposite *The political candidates were each sticking to their respective platforms which were the antithesis of one another.*

assess (v.) to evaluate *After the party, we went to assess the damage to the room – it was not pretty.*

cliché (n.) overused expression, commonplace expression *His cliché expressions were exasperating – yes, we know, "That's the way the ball bounces."*

enigmatic (adj.) mystifying, hard to figure out *The enigmatic man was a mystery even to those who knew him well.*

complement (v.) to go along with well; to complete *That tie definitely complements that suit. You should get compliments on it.*

consensus (n.) an agreement of opinion, a group opinion that is agreed upon *A consensus is different than a vote – everyone agrees to compromise and present one opinion.*

demure (adj.) quiet, modest, reserved, soft-spoken *Debbie remained demure at the frat party while others went crazy.*

ossify (v.) to become fixed and inflexible in one's opinions, rocklike *When presented with the FOSSIL, he was ossified in his believe that it was in fact an old car part.*

Parts of the Whole

constituent (n.) an important part *In the early twentieth century, fish scales were a constituent part of lipstick.*

eclectic (adj.) made up of diverse elements *His electric guitar collection is very eclectic – he has guitars from seven different countries.*

convention 1. (n.) an assembly of like-minded or like-employed *There is usually not much rule-breaking at the Grammarian's Convention* 2. (n.) a rule, custom, standard *It was a convention at the convention that no one misplace a modifier.*

multifarious (adj.) very diverse in makeup, having a great many sides or facets *My new car is multifarious; it can fly, swim, and drive.*

criteria (n.) standards by which something is judged or chosen *The criteria for a good novel include: plot, character, and flow quality.*

dearth (n.) a lack, scarcity, shortage *What's a dearth worth? The potato dearth of the 1800's killed one-third of the population. The dearth caused death.*

palette (adj.) range of colors, qualities, or styles *The artist used a large palette to create the beautiful portrait.*

disparate (adj.) sharply differing, containing sharply contrasting elements, very varied in makeup *Although we all saw the same play, we have disparate opinions.*

elicit (v.) to bring forth, draw out, to get *No matter how many times I talked to my pet rock, I was never able to elicit a response.*

overmorrow (n.) the day after tomorrow *Come over tomorrow, or, overmorrow at the latest!.*

NOTES

People That Help or Hurt

arbiter (n.) someone who resolves disputes, an intermediary *The court assigned an arbiter to hear our dispute and rule on it.*

clergy (n.) members of Christian holy orders *He had wanted to be a clergyman ever since he was a boy, so he signed up at the seminary when he was old enough.*

swagger (n.) boastful presence, haughtiness *He walked with such swagger all I could do is laugh – he looked ridiculous.*

artisan (n.) craftsman *The artisan created a beautiful table for our living room.*

ascetic (adj.) restraint as a means of self-discipline, usually religious *The ascetic monk showed his devotion by living in a small room with nothing but a sleeping mat.*

cobbler (n.) 1. a person who makes or repairs shoes *It was sad when the only cobbler in town retired, it felt like an era was over.* 2. dessert made from soft fruit *My mother's peach cobbler is superb.*

arrogant (adj.) braggy, bold, annoying, haughty *His arrogant manner really turned people off – after a while, he had no friends.*

supercilious (adj.) thinking one is better than others, arrogant *The supercilious professor turned off his entire class.*

detrimental (adj.) harmful or having a negative effect on *Taking drugs is detrimental to one's health. You would have to be MENTAL to do it.*

condolence (n.) expression of sympathy over a death or deaths *He came to the house an expressed his sincere condolences when he heard our friend had died.*

vociferous (adj.) loud, noisy, unruly *I was sick of the vociferous arguments we had nightly, so we broke up.*

condone (v.) to support or deliberately overlook a misdeed *By not reporting his crime, you are condoning his actions.*

decorous (adj.) socially proper, appropriate, well-behaved *The teenager was remarkably decorous for one raised in the streets.*

confidant (n.) a person entrusted with secrets, a best friend *In Harry Potter, Sirius was Harry's confidant – he knew all his secrets.*

Secrets

covert (adj.) secretly engaged in, done in a hidden manner *He covertly planned his attack – no one knew it was coming.*

delineate (v.) to describe, outline, shed light on, explain *The mayor delineated the plan for the town. He drew the LINES.*

cryptic (adj.) secretive, hard to figure out *His cryptic message had us all wondering what the heck he was talking about. He was in a secret crypt???*

debunk (v.) to expose the falseness of *He debunked the notion that she was the best tennis player in the world by beating her three straight matches.*

timorous (adj.) timid, fearful, shy *Timorous Timothy would cry whenever he met someone new.* Timorous Timothy – the shy guy.

foresight (n.) ability to see what's ahead, wise view of probable events *His father was known for his foresight, for he could tell we were going to hold a party when he went away on vacation!*

candid (adj.) expressing pure honesty without the hint of deception *I found her candid statement very endearing. I did not know she felt that way.*

erroneous (adj.) wrong *His argument that the world was flat turned out to be erroneous.*

NOTES

Should I?

chronicle 1. (n.) a written history *The chronicle of the period was extensive and intereresting.* 2. (v.) to write a history *They chronicled our trip so well that re-reading it felt like revisiting it.*

abstain (v.) to choose not to do something *The unsure legislator abstained from the controversial vote.*

constrain (v.) to hold back, forcibly restrict *His incredibly bad singing voice constrained him from joining the chorus.*

annex 1. (v.) to incorporate territory or space into one's own holdings *We annexed the coffee shop next door when it closed down as we needed more space for our warehouse.*

burnish (v.) to polish, shine up *He burnished the hood of the car until it gleamed in the sunlight.*

annul (v.) to make void or invalid, to cancel *The marriage was annulled when it turned out the groom was already married.*

fabricate (v.) to make up, invent *He fabricated a story so believable the professor accepted it.*

consign (v.) to give over to another's care or use *He finally gave in, and consigned his father to a nursing home.*

espouse (v.) to support, join in support of *I espouse animal rights since I love all animals.*

appropriate (v.) to take, make use of *Quoting "eminent domain," the town appropriated the land next to the highway for expansion.*

embellish 1. (v.) to decorate, add detail to, enhance. *When she returned from the movie and said it was "fun," I asked her to embellish.*

dissuade (v.) to persuade not to do something *I tried to dissuade my sister from going out in the rain, but she did not listen.* DISSUADE jacket? No way! Don't wear that!

compensate (v.) to make payment for something as per its value, not as an outright purchase (something broken or taken) *When the waiter spilled wine on my wife's white dress, the manager quickly offered to compensate us for the cost of the dress.*

deliberate (adj.) intentional, showing careful planning and thought *His actions were deliberate although he denied planning them in advance.*

deface (v.) to ruin or damage something's appearance *The scofflaws used paint to deface the building's exterior.*

impinge 1. (v.) to impact, affect, , encroach upon *I hate to ask, but I must impinge upon you to use your restroom. Quickly!*

cleave 1. (v.) to divide into parts, or physically cut *They boys cleaved into two teams.* 2. (v.) to stick together in a hard manner *The bad storm cleaved the men together for survival.*

advocate 1. (v.) to argue for something *Max advocated pizza, although we all wanted Chinese food.* 2. (n.) one who argues for something *Max is always a pizza advocate. Can't get that guy to eat moo-shoo.*

immerse (v.) to absorb oneself in *When I discovered the famous author, I was immersed in his works for weeks.*

impetuous (adj.) done with little thought or planning, reckless *Giving the finger to the cop was an impetuous move.*

punctilious (adj.) willing to follow rules or standards *Our hall monitor was so punctilious we named him "Captain Annoying."*

nurture (v.) to help the development of; to train and tutor *We nurture our children by teaching them the ways of the world.*

remiss (adj.) negligent, failing to take care or do something assigned *The cat got out when the maid, remiss in her duties, failed to close the back door.*

exhort (v.) to urge, prod, encourage *Katherine exhorted Aviv to be nicer to Dave or pay the price.*

repose (v.) to rest, lie down, take a break *The dog reposed on the cool lawn after it was watered on a very hot day.*

calibrate (v.) to set standard, mark for measurement *We calibrated the bottle so we could measure the exact amount of liquid in it.*

yoke (v.) to join, link together *The ropes were yoked by a larger rope wrapped around them.* Seeing them tied together was a real YOKE.

NOTES

Size Matters

colossus (n.) a gigantic thing *I love the colossus that marks the entrance to the town.*

capacious (adj.) large and open, very spacious *His open floor plan made for a capacious living area off the kitchen.*

daunting (adj.) intimidating, causing one to lose courage, huge in scope (like a task) *The haunting was daunting as we had so much to carry.*

grandiose (adj.) on a magnificent or exaggerated scale, huge, grand *The grandiose celebration required over two hundred workers to organize.*

copious – (adj.) large amount, huge *Copious amounts of burgers were enjoyed at the barbeque.*

meager (adj.) very small in size or quality *Usually gourmet restaurants serve very meager portions.*

commodious (adj.) big, roomy *The minivan's commodious back seats allowed the entire team to ride together.*

corpulence (adj.) obesity, extreme fatness *His weekend of binge eating added to his already impressive corpulence.*

wane – (verb) to get smaller, diminish *I watched as his influence over the group began to wane.* My friend WANE is the smallest guy I know and keeps getting smaller!

diminutive (adj.) tiny, delicate, miniature *The older student picked on the diminutive freshman.*

saturate (v.) to completely fill, usually with liquid *The sponge was saturated, so it could not hold any more water.*

tenable (adj.) able to be defended or maintained; usable *His argument, on a scale of 1 to 10, was usable, therefore tenable.*

emaciated (adj.) very thin, unhealthy looking *The model looked emaciated, not thin and sexy.*

distend (v.) to swell outward *Beer drinking tends to distend the stomach – DIS TENDS to make you look fat.*

Skills and Talents

acumen (n.) insight, shrewdness *Her business acumen made her a star in the corporate world.*

clairvoyant (adj.) able to perceive things that normal people cannot *He claimed he was clairvoyant, but he could never pick lottery numbers, so I didn't believe him.*

fathom (v.) to understand, comprehend, figure out *I cannot fathom why you enjoy the company of that nasty person.*

arcane (adj.) obscure, secret, known only by a few, magical *The professor of Greek DiningWare taught a most arcane subject.*

cogent (adj.) intellectually convincing *Her arguments were extremely cogent – it was obvious she knew her stuff.*

remedial (adj.) intended to repair gaps in one's basic knowledge *After failing algebra, I was enrolled in a remedial math class.*

expedient (adj.) positive, serving one's own self-interest, beneficial *After almost going bankrupt, the company made many expedient moves which brought it back to market prominence.* Going to EXPEDIENT.COM will help you travel to better things for yourself.

eminent 1. (adj.) distinguished, prominent, famous *Written by an eminent scholar in the field, Professor Dave's books have helped thousands of students.*

perspicacity (adj.) shrewdness, perceptiveness, especially in business or negotiation *The queen was noted for her perspicacity dealing with other dignitaries.*

legerdemain (n.) deception, slight-of-hand, fooling the eye with physical prowess *Sneaking vodka into the ballgame in a container shaped like binoculars was a brilliant piece of legerdemain.*

rhapsodize (v.) to speak overly enthusiastically *I rhapsodized about their new album since I thought it was so awesome.*

temerity (n.) audacity, recklessness, headstrongness *His temerity prevented him from turning down any dare, no matter how dangerous or silly.*

uncanny (adj.) of supernatural character or origin, hard to believe as real, extraordinary *His ability to predict what others would do was uncanny. He seemed to be inside their heads.*

ingenious (adj.) very smart or clever; extremely useful *Since I'm allergic to peanuts, the chef's ingenious use of walnuts to make the snack mix was greatly appreciated.*

adroit (adj.) skillful, talented *The adroit shortstop made the throw look effortless.*

temperance (n.) moderation in doing or thinking; level-headedness *His natural temperance made him an excellent leader.*

agile (adj.) quick, nimble *The agile kitten deftly avoided the boy's reach.*

meritorious (adj.) worthy of reward *The soldiers were given meritorious recognition for their part in the battle.*

perplex (v.) to utterly confuse *The math problems on the mid-term perplexed the students.*

accessible (adj.) obtainable, reachable *Learning vocabulary can lead to high scores which can make higher level colleges accessible.*

impervious (adj.) impenetrable, can't be affected by *Penguins are impervious to the bitter cold of the Arctic Ocean.*

acclaim (n.) high praise *The band's new song was a hit and met with critical acclaim.*

discern (v.) to perceive, detect, or figure out *Her smack of my face helped me discern she did not want to be kissed.*

assiduous (adj.) hard-working, attentive to detail *His assiduous labor paid off as the statue looked wonderful.*

captivate (v.) to hold the attention of *The sight of the whales off the side of the boat captivated everyone on board.*

astute (adj.) clever, crafty *His astute answers helped him win the debate.*

bard (n.) a poet, a singer *The bard at the inn made the night a beautiful experience.*

NOTES

Shall We Argue?

upbraid (v.) to criticize or scold severely *The police officer upbraided the man for running the red light because he was on his cell phone.*

deprecate (v.) to belittle, to criticize *He deprecated the new employee for his lack of concern.*

castigate (v.) to scold or punish harshly *The cast of the play was castigated by the director for the actor's poor performance.*

rebuke (v.) to scold, criticize *The poet was rebuked for using passages taken directly from another poet.*

impertinent (adj.) rude or inappropriate *His impertinent comments were typical of his nasty personality.*

reprove (v.) to scold, verbally reprimand *The young man was reproved by his boss for drinking beer at lunchtime. He could not PROVE otherwise.*

berate (v.) to scream at; chastise *He berated her for hours, and I felt terrible for her.*

contentious (adj.) argumentative, liking dispute *Sean said my contentious manner was tough to take; I was always looking to argue.*

repudiate (v.) to reject, refuse to accept or argue against *He repudiated my claim that I was part lizard until he saw my tail.*

censure 1. (v.) to criticize or rebuke harshly *The professor was censured for inappropriate jokes during class.*

dissent 1. (v.,n.) to disagree , disagreement *We voiced our dissent to the landlord and he fixed the broken pipes without charging us.*

rail (v.) to scold, protest, or argue about *He railed about the inequity in the seniority system, but to no avail.*

disputatious (adj.) prone to arguing, liking arguments and dissention *She was so disputatious that one could not go three minutes without screaming at her.*

concede (v.) to accept as true *She presented such a strong argument I was forced to concede her point.*

promulgate (v.) to proclaim, make known *The principal promulgated that the prom would be canceled due to the security concerns.*

coherent (adj.) logically consistent, intelligible *I could not figure out what the very upset girl was saying – her statements were not coherent.*

captious (adj.) prone to arguing *His captious nature meant he was constantly fighting with everyone.*

polemical (adj.) prone to arguing, controversial, in dispute *The rules of the dorm were polemical – no one wanted to follow them.*

carp (v.) to find fault with *He carped our plans to catch carp – apparently he didn't like the taste of the fish.*

chastise (v.) to criticize severely *The young child was chastised for running into the street.*

impugn (v.) to insult or criticize *The mayor's plan to restore the block was impugned by the locals as impractical and wasteful.*

rebuff (v.) to verbally deny, go against *He was rebuffed by his training coach for trying to become buff.*

vehemently (adv.) acting or speaking with intense force or emotion *The man vehemently denied being present at the robbery.*

counteract (v.) to neutralize, make ineffective *The cough medicine counteracted his bad cough.*

Tell Me About It

arid (adj.) excessively dry *The Sahara Desert is one of the most arid places on Earth. The "Sarahid"*

lithe (adj.) flexible, supple, graceful in movement *The ballet performers with incredibly lithe.*

elaborate (adj.) complex, detailed *His elaborate guitar playing is always a treat for the ears.*

limpid (adj.) clear, transparent, usually used metaphorically *His limpid essay style made his works easy to understand.*

variegated (adj.) distinct in marking, varied *Each theatre in the multiplex was variegated bya different color to make it easier to find the one a particular movie was playing in.*

florid (adj.) flowery, ornate, decorated *The florid room made my senses reel.*

hypothetical (adj.) unproven, vague, supposed *The man described the horrors of war by using hypothetical battle situations.*

indigenous (adj.) from a particular area *Palm trees are not indigenous to New York.*

subtle (adj.) not out in the open, suggested, hinted at *The subtle urgings of his parents finally took hold, and he studied much more than he used to.*

hardy (adj.) robust, capable of surviving despite hardship *The adverse weather did not affect the hardy plants.*

tangential (adj.) incidental, peripheral, divergent from the main focus *When discussing his grades, the student kept bringing up tangential subjects to stray from the main topic.* As in math, a TANGENT goes off to the side.

pacific (adj.) soothing, calming in manner *The pacific counselor was a huge help in calming the upset students after the incident at the school.*

evanescent (adj.) fleeting, momentary, brief *My joy was evanescent; After receiving the high grade I was assigned extra work by the professor.*

folly (n.) inability to look ahead, silly view of the future, silliness *Buying a boat before he moved to the coast was pure folly.*

substantiate (v.) to back up, support *His argument was substantiated by the evidence he brought forth.*

epitome (n.) the perfect example of, embodiment *My sister, the epitome of good taste, always dresses fabulously.*

Things and Stuff

laceration (n.) a cut or tear *His lacerations from falling off his bike were very severe.*

encumber (v.) to weigh down or burden *I was encumbered with both mine and my wife's suitcases.*

zephyr (n.) a light breeze *The nightly zephyrs made the environment very pleasant.*

inexorable (adj.) incapable of being persuaded or calmed *I asked to go to the movies with my friends for a week – my father was inexorable and wouldn't let me go.*

anecdote (n.) a short, humorous story, usually with a point or lesson *My anecdote about swimming with the angry dolphins is a favorite of all who hear it.*

aisle (n.) a passageway between rows of seats *The aisle was too narrow for Charlene to navigate in her wheelchair.*

superfluous (adj.) exceeding what is necessary, extra *Dessert was superfluous after the huge meal she had served us.*

tantamount (adj.) equal to *The old car was costing him so much money I explained that paying for repairs was tantamount to making a new car payment.*

potable (adj.) drinkable *When walking in the desert, it is vital to bring enough potable water along.*

linchpin (n.) something holding separate parts together, a unifying force *Since no one would go to the party unless Dave was going, he was implored by the host to come – he was the linchpin of the party.*

parody (n.) an imitation to make a point, usually using satire *When the teacher walked in, Scott didn't notice her and continued his parody of her teaching style. He's in detention now.*

morass (n.) a wet swampy bog; or something that traps and confuses *The fiscal morass the company found itself in would take years to improve.*

nadir (n.) the lowest point *The nadir of my week came when the air conditioner at work broke.*

reciprocate (v.) to give in return for something received *She reciprocated my kind words with kind words of her own.*

salve (n.) a soothing cream or healing balm *The sunburn salve helped the pain quite a bit.*

pathology (n.) deviation from normal; disease *His pathology was hard to identify, no one could tell just what was wrong with him.*

vicarious (adj.) experiencing something through someone else *Many little leaguers suffer because of the vicarious desires of their parents wanting to play major league baseball.*

hiatus (n.) a break (in a timeline or job) *Because of its seasonal business, the staff gets a nice hiatus each winter.*

respite (n.) a break, rest *When the mailman finally left, Sophie took a respite from her mad barking.*

mandate (n.) command from a higher authority *The skating rink manager mandated that ice fishing is not allowed.*

artifact (n.) surviving piece from an extinct people or place *Scientists can study ancient cultures by examining their artifacts.*

altercation (n.) fight, scuffle *The men were so angry an altercation was sure to happen.* Don't fight in church – that would be an ALTARcation.

reservoir 1. (n.) reserves, large supply, especially of water *His internal reservoir of strength was demonstrated as he swam effortlessly across the reservoir.*

mores (n.) moral attitudes and fixed customs of a group *Television mores change all the time; in the 1950's, Lucy and her husband were not allowed to appear to sleep in the same bed in the hit show "I Love Lucy".*

anomaly (n.) an unusual occurrence, something out of the ordinary *Because of the odds involved, winning the lottery can only be described as an anomaly.*

asylum 1. (n.) a place of refuge, sanctuary *His room was his asylum; no one bothered him once he was inside.* 2. (n.) place where the insane are kept *Although technically NOT so, most high schools are called asylums.*

battery 1.(n.) a portable power device *The flashlight did not work because it did not have a battery.* 2. (n.)assault, beating *When he hit the other patron, he was charged with battery.*

cadence (n.) a rhythm or beat *The drummer's right foot provided a steady cadence for the rest of the band.*

behemoth (n.) something huge or powerful *The new Boeing 787 is a true behemoth of the sky.*

catalog 1. (v.) to list, or enter into a list *The lawyers cataloged the assets to ensure a fair distribution.* 2. (n.) a list or collection *The catalog of shoes arrived in the mail.*

labyrinth (n.) a very confusing or complex maze *The old building was a labyrinth of corridors – we were lost for hours.*

turmoil (n.) confusing situation or attitude *The fire alarm at three a.m. had everyone in turmoil.*

compound 1. (v.) to combine *He compounded his problems by having too much to drink.* 2. (n.) a combination of different parts *It was a compound problem brought about by his parents, his sister, and his friends.* 3. (n.) a walled area containing buildings *In the movie "The Godfather", the family takes safety in their private compound.*

NOTES

To Do, or Not To Do

prescribe (v.) to clearly state a rule or policy *The manager prescribed the new no-smoking policy.*

surfeit (n.) an oversupply or large indulgence *The surfeit of cake at dinner made me very sorry later, for my stomach was upset all night.*

recapitulate (v.) to review or repeat, to sum up *He recapitulated the entire month's doings in preparation for the policy change.*

surmise (v.) to guess or speculate with little evidence *After hearing both vastly different accounts of the fight, he was able to surmise what truly took place.*

canvas 1. (n.) a piece of cloth for painting Leonardo Da Vinci painted on many surfaces in addition to canvas. 2. (v.) to cover with questions, inspect *The detectives canvassed the neighborhood seeking clues to the killer's identity.*

juxtapose (v.) placing two things next to each other for comparison *We laid the floor tile samples on the table for juxtaposition.*

extricate (v.) to disentangle (Instead of trying to mediate between my brother and sister, I extricated myself from the family tension entirely and left the house for the day.)

expurgate (v.) to remove offensive or incorrect parts, usually of a book or other written work *When it was determined the story was inaccurate, the editor expurgated it from the text.*

implacable (adj.) can't be calmed down or made to feel better about something *When he canceled the date at the last minute, she was implacable.*

irrevocable (adj.) can't be taken back *The mayor ensured the pollution law was irrevocable.*

subjugate (v.) to bring under control, subdue, put down *During World War II, the Nazis were able to subjugate Paris very quickly.*

fetter (v.) to chain up or restrain *We left our beloved Rosie fettered to the parking meter.*

evince (v.) to show, reveal *His nail-biting and pacing evinced his nervousness about the exam.*

exigent (adj.) urgent, very important *Our need for water was exigent, we were risking severe dehydration.*

attribute 1. (v.) to credit to, *I attribute my success as a writer to the reading I did as a child.* 2. (n.) an element of oneself or trait *His attributes made him a natural athelete.*

adamant (adj.) keeps going, does not give up *The professor was adamant that his theory was correct even in the face of evidence to the contrary.*

adhere 1. (n.) to stick to – virtually or actually *We adhered to our plan to adhere stickers to every car in the parking lot.*

adumbrate (v.) to sketch out in a vague or unclear way *The bandleader adumbrated the next set, but no one knew for sure what songs we would play.*

abstemious (adj.) to hold back from eating or drinking too much *When he finally learned to be abstemious, he lost weight rapidly.* Abstain! Be ABSTEMIUOS.

renunciation (n.) to reject outright something previously done *His renunciation of smoking greatly improved his health.*

enthrall (v.) to charm, hold spellbound *My stories of near-misses in the tower always hold the audience enthralled.*

ambivalent (adj.) having opposing feelings, uncertainty *I am ambivalent about Mike – he is my dear friend but he is a very mean person sometimes.*

appraise (v.) to determine the value of *The insurance company held onto the ring so it could properly appraise it.*

aspire (v.) to long for, aim toward, want *He aspires to be CEO of the company one day.*

compress (v.) to apply pressure, squeeze together, to push *I compressed the sandwich to the point it started leaking out of the sides.*

To Thine Own Self Be True

abnegation (n.) intentionally keeping oneself uncomfortable, denied of comfort. *Practicing abnegation, the monk slept on the cold cement floor.*

credulity (n.) readiness or willingness to believe *Her credulity made her an easy target for smooth talkers.*

acquiesce (v.) to agree to easily, go along with *Although I prefer golf, I acquiesced to a game of tennis.*

propensity (n.) a preference towards, leaning towards *Rosie, my dog, has a propensity for barking.*

equanimity (n.) calmness and composure *The air traffic controller watched the busy radar screen with his typical professional equanimity.*

incontrovertible (adj.) indisputable, absolutely true *The fact that the Earth revolves around the sun is incontrovertible – but this was not always the case.* When I drive my INCONVTROVERTIBLE I am forced to tell the truth!

maverick (n.) independent, nonconformist *Doug never went along with the crowd, for he is a true maverick.* The MAVERICK horse never followed the others.

conformist (n.) person who behaves the same as other people or "goes along with the crowd" *Charlie was known as a conformist since he would do whatever his friends did.*

diffident (adj.) shy, quiet, modest *While dining in the restaurant, the young boy was diffident and polite.* A shy person is DIFFIDENT than a rude one.

fidelity (n.) loyalty, devotion *German Shepard dogs are known for their fidelity towards their masters.*

hapless (adj.) habitually unlucky *Our hapless group always seems to pick a rainy day to go fishing.*

divulge (v.) to verbally reveal something *With intense pressure from the press, the politician finally divulged his secret.*

idiosyncratic (adj.) characteristic of one person; highly individualized or specialized *Since the writing errors were so idiosyncratic, I knew who the "anonymous" author was.*

oblivious (adj.) lacking awareness *We were oblivious to the burning smell coming from the kitchen, and the cake was ruined.*

pathos (n.) sympathy *The hurt dog filled me with pathos as I tried to help him.*

spurious (adj.) false but made to seem real or believable *His argument was spurious, but so well delivered people were obviously believing it.*

obdurate (adj.) unyielding to pressure to change views or morals *Despite the situation, the obdurate teacher would not postpone the assignment's due date.*

veracity (n.) truthfulness, accuracy *The veracity of his accusations was demonstrated clearly by the documents he submitted.*

probity (n.) virtue, integrity, truthfulness *Abraham Lincoln is often referred to as a man of great probity.*

penitent (adj.) remorseful, regretful, humble *The penitent man is humble before his deity.*

insurgent (n.) a rebel *The insurgent refused to sit down as directed, and disrupted the entire session.*

idolatrous (adj.) worshipping one object or person to excess *Victor's idolatrous following of Bruce Springsteen was borderline stalking.*

induce (v.) to bring about, stimulate to start *His constant screaming induced a panic in the crowd, and people started to flee.*

candor (n.) honesty, frankness *Usually difficult to figure out, the governor's speech was filled with surprising candor.*

innate (adj.) inborn, native, inside one's self *Although he does not work out, his innate talent makes him one of the best players on the team.*

ingenuous (adj.) innocent and true *His speech was so ingenuous he won over many new supporters; you could tell it came right from his heart.*

obstinate (adj.) stubborn, unyielding *His obstinacy was legendary, for he could not be swayed once his mind was made up.*

analogous (adj.) similar to, or the same as *The DNA of a human is quite analogous to that of the chimpanzee.*

anonymous (adj.) unknown, unrecognized, unidentified *The anonymous donor gave over ten thousand dollars to the charity.*

bashful (adj.) very shy *When encountering someone you like, it's easy to become bashful.*

camaraderie (n.) brotherhood, unity, friendship *The camaraderie among the army unit was impressive to observe, they were like brothers.*

NOTES

Utter Destruction

conflagration (n.) huge fire *The conflagration could be seen for miles. Burning a large number of flags would cause a conFLAGration.*

raze (v.) to completely destroy, clear, or demolish *The old building was razed to make room for the new park.* Every morning I try not to destroy my face with a RAZER.

debacle (n.) a horrible failure, disruption *His barbeque turned into a debacle when the burgers caught fire.*

desecrate (v.) violate the sacredness of a thing or place, to destroy the peace *The cement structure in the middle of the field desecrated the peaceful scene.*

chaos (n.) complete and utter disorder *When the attack first came, the town was plunged into chaos. People were running everywhere panicking.*

desolate (adj.) deserted, dreary, lifeless *The desolate landscape after the bomb hit made it clear no one had survived.*

despair (n.) extreme sadness, hopelessness *Despair gripped the pair as they realized the ship was sinking and there was nothing they could do about it.*

despondent (adj.) feeling depressed, discouraged, hopeless *John was despondent when they gave the job to someone else.*

NOTES

Whatever You Say

sycophant (n.) one who flatters for self-gain, obsequious *He agreed with everything I said, even the crazy stuff, he was a true sycophant.*

obsequious (adj.) compliant or submissive to an annoying or phony level *The obsequious waiter was so annoying we took another table away from him.*

corroborate (v.) to support, to go along with, show evidence that goes along with *His crazy story was corroborated by witnesses.*

subservient (adj.) obedient *It was sad to watch how subservient she was to her boyfriend – he ordered her around like a slave.*

fawn (v.) to gain acceptance or favor by flattering someone *Roger fawned over her so much she agreed to go out with him.*

submissive (adj.) giving in to others *The image of the submissive wife of the 1950's is practically gone in this country.*

conundrum (n.) puzzle, problem, difficult situation *Since he had two invitations for the same night, he flipped a coin to solve the conundrum.*

blandish (v.) to entice by using flattery *The managers blandished the vendors hoping to make a deal.*

subordinate (n.) lower in rank, lower in status *His subordinates thought very highly of him because of his fairness of a manager.*

submissive (adj.) giving in to others *The image of the submissive wife of the 1950's is practically gone in this country.*

compliant (adj.) adapting to another's wishes *We were compliant with the wishes of the staff and moved our Great Dane outside.*

servile (adj.) subservient *The servile waitress looked intimidated by her customers as she bowed at each table.*

toady (n.) sycophantic, subservient for gain *He was such a toady even the coach got sick of it and threw him off the team.*

concomitant (adj.) obeying and accompanying, going along with as a servant *I agreed to be concomitant for a week if I lost the bet.*

decry (v.) to criticize openly and strongly *The town decried the fee charged by the town crier – it was simply too much. Decried the crier.*

congruity (n.) being in agreement, on equal terms *The players reached a congruity with the owners and signed the new contract. (If only CONGRESS could reach CONGRUITY)*

construe (v.) to interpret, understand *The gas light, the sputtering engine, and the slowing of the vehicle allowed Skip to construe he was out of gas.*

abstruse (adj.) hard to understand *I have always found Physics to be abstruse.*

curt (adj.) abruptly and rudely short in speech or manner *No one likes my friend Kurt; people think he's rude because of his one word answers.*

dispassionate *(adj.)* Not affected by emotion. Stolid. *His dispassionate nature made him the perfect choice to lead the group in the emotional battle.*

Wordiness or Lack Thereof

laconic (adj.) brief and precise in speech or writing *The tremendously long novel could have benefited from some laconic chapters.*

voluble (adj.) speaking easily, glib *His voluble manner made him very popular.*

eloquent (adj.) expressive, articulate, moving with speech *His speech was so eloquent the students were rapt with attention.*

rant (n.) a rapidly delivered complaining speech *His rant was crazy – he went on and on about everything.*

quiescent (adj.) quiet, still, not active *Her normally quiescent manner abruptly ended when she was angered by his statement.*

concise (adj.) short, brief and direct in expression *Due to the limited time, he gave us concise instructions as to how to proceed.*

colloquial (adj.) informal form of conversation, everyday speech *Colloquial style does not belong in most essays.*

succinct (adj.) compact and precise *His essay was succinct, covering everything in a single page.*

digress *(v.)* to stray off topic, wander verbally *When someone says "I digress," you're usually bored already.*

brevity (n.) quickness, briefness *His explanation was full of brevity, for he gave no unnecessary details.*

taciturn (adj.) not talkative, shy *Jennifer is quite talkative, unlike her taciturn brother.*

loquacious (adj.) very talkative, never shuts up *My friend LOQUASHA is so loquacious none of us gets a word in edgewise.*

pithy (adj.) brief, short, but meaningful *Usually pithy, his explanation went on for long minutes.*

reticent (adj.) not speaking much, quiet *Getting the whole story from the reticent witness was quite a task.*

terse (adj.) short, bulleted in speech *The drill sergeant's terse manner was very effective.*

verbose (adj.) wordy, overly long in speech *His explanation was extremely verbose, it seems to me he could have summed it all up in two sentences.*

rhetoric (n.) clever, short, effective speech *His gift for rhetoric made him fans wherever he spoke.*

grandiloquence (n.) lofty, pompous language *His grandiloquent style made him sound like an idiot in the end.*

bombastic (adj.) excessively wordy, pompous in speech *Speaking bombastically, he simply sounded like an idiot. He didn't even use the fancy words correctly.*

circumlocution (n.) indirect and wordy language *The politician's statement can only be described as circumlocution – he went round and round and round.*

garrulous (adj.) talkative, wordy, never shuts up *My friend GARRY is so garrulous he never shuts up.*

prattle (n.) silly, foolish talk *His speech was so filled with prattle people started to boo.*

diffuse 1. (v.) to scatter about or thin out in concentration *His clever joke diffused the tension in the room.*

ramble (v.) to speak without order, to go on and on without direction *His speech rambled so much I found myself falling asleep.*

gregarious (adj.) drawn to be with people, sociable *Those that are gregarious are seldom lonely*

jocular (adj.) friendly, funny, liking to be around others *Jack was so friendly we called him "Jocular Jack."*

Yawn. I've Heard It All Before

insipid (adj.) dull and/or boring *His writing is so insipid I cannot read more than two or three pages before falling asleep.*

phlegmatic (adj.) uninterested, unresponsive, slow *His phlegmatic response was so atypical we worried something was seriously wrong with him.*

derivative (adj.) taken from another source, unoriginal *Her friend's band was too derivative for her taste – it sounded like every other band she had heard.*

trite (adj.) unoriginal, overused *His jokes were very trite since he took them from the joke pages of the local newspaper.*

remote (adj.) distant, physically or emotionally *His remote manner when asked for the remote was interesting. He said it was so far away, so remote, that he did not even remotely care about it.*

mundane (adj.) regular, commonplace, standard, not exciting *The show was quite mundane; we could tell what was about to happen before it did.*

nonchalant (adj.) having a lack of concern, indifference, casual *When his girlfriend, Chalant, asked him for a favor, he acted as if he didn't care. He is now NONCHALANT.*

apathetic (adj.) lacking concern or emotion, not caring Carl was apathetic about politics – he felt it didn't matter who was in office.

listless (adj.) showing no energy, not caring, slow *He had to make a list – but he was so listless – he made no list. He didn't have the energy.*

platitude (n.) an uninspired remark, cliché saying After coming home late, I knew I would have to listen to my parent's platitudes, which was worse than going to the dentist.

hackneyed (adj.) unoriginal, overused, trite *After his hackneyed cries of "wolf," we stopped responding.*

lackluster (adj.) nothing special, plain, ordinary *The lackluster book left almost no impression on me, for it was nothing special.*

impassive (adj.) unemotional, not giving in to emotion, especially suffering *Impassiveness is fine, but it's okay to cry once in a while.*

prosaic (adj.) plain, ordinary *Most mosaic is NOT prosaic – it is interesting and beautiful.*

vapid (adj.) boring, dull, plain *His poem was vapid, although we had expected it to be exciting and fresh.*

aloof (adj.) reserved, distant, not warm *The aloof professor was nevertheless loved by his students.*

detached (adj.) not caring, indifferent *The man was detached from the movie – and if he didn't pay attention – things would become DETACHED from him by his girlfriend...*

indifferent (adj.) showing no care or concern *He was indifferent as to whether we had pizza or hot wings.*

stolid (adj.) expressing little emotion *I knew better – but her stolid manner at the funeral made some people think she did not care.*

ambiguous (adj.) uncertain, having more than one possible meaning *Some clever advertising is intentionally ambiguous – having double meanings.*

banal (adj.) dull, commonplace, boring *The last book I read was quite banal, so I would not recommend it.*

capricious (adj.) whimsical, , fickle, changing one's mind rapidly and without apparent reason *Her capricious nature was charming at times, but it could also be annoying.*

jaded (adj.) unconcerned due to overexposure to something *The fireman has been to so many awful scenes he has become jaded to them.*

tedious (adj.) dull, boring, repetitive in a negative way *Mowing the lawn became so tedious last summer I paid a neighbor to do it.*

dispassionate (adj.) unaffected by emotion *His passionate relationship ended because he was too dispassionate; he just didn't care.*

Yuck!

rancid (adj.) having terrible taste or smell *The cheese that had fallen behind the refrigerator was so rancid, we had to throw out the entire block.*

debauchery (n.) corruption by sensual pleasure, bad behavior, deviant treatment *His outright debauchery at the party earned him a suspension at work. Taking naked photos of himself and posting them on the wall was not a good idea.*

corrosive (adj.) having the ability to erode or eat away *Salt water is notoriously corrosive to boat bottoms.*

anathema (n.) a hated, detested person *My high school English teacher called me an anathema – I guess sleeping with his wife was a problem.*

distend – (verb) to swell out, stick out *The broken bone caused her entire arm to distend.* My belly was so huge it went from DISTEND to DATEND.

contusion (n.) bruise, injury, break *After the accident, he had contusions on his arms for several weeks.*

dissemble (v.) to hid or conceal, fake *To get out of the school assembly, we dissembled illness, but it did not work.*

cacophony (n.) loud sound, harsh sound, loud crash *The youth choir was a true cacophony – but the children were so cute it didn't matter.*

virulent (adj.) extremely dangerous or harmful *The virulent virus wiped out have of the village's population.*

fetid (adj.) smells terrible *The lunchbox that had not been opened in months began to emit a fetid odor – we were afraid to open it.*

precarious (adj.) risky, dangerous, not on solid ground *The precarious position of the antennae on the roof made us wonder when it would fall.*

gratuitous (adj.) uncalled for, unnecessary excess *The guy at Burger King gave me an gratuitous amount of ketchup – I could bathe in it if I wanted to.*

aggrieved (adj.) distressed, wronged, pissed-off *The aggrieved customer really let the manager have it.*

pejorative (adj.) negative in content, uncomplimentary *His tone was pejorative; he was obviously not pleased with our efforts.*

aversion (n.) a dislike for something *His aversion to flying kept him from travelling anywhere that required taking an airplane.*

predatory (adj.) taking advantage of others, using others for one's own gain *The predatory nature of the lion is well know – what is not well know is that people can be just as predatory.*

irreverence (n.) disrespect *His irreverence at the meeting caused the others to ask him to leave.*

anxiety (n.) intense uneasiness *His anxiety before the test was unwarranted; he was prepared.*

privation (n.) lacking basic needs or requirements *The privation of the "Spartan Resort" did not appeal to me – I like fluffy robes and room service.*

unctuous (adj.) smooth, but in a greasy way – used car salesman-ish – *Right away I could sense he was unctuous – only being polite because he thought we were wealthy.*

caustic (adj.) bitter, biting, nasty *The two lawyers refused to get closer than two feet from one another, but they exchanged enough caustic insults to last a lifetime.*

odious (adj.) causing hatred or ill feelings *Cleaning up after the party was a necessary but odious task.* Cleaning a commodious is really kinda odious.

maudlin (adj.) sentimental from weakness or overreaction *The film was quite maudlin, filled with shallow characters in predictable situations.* My friend MAUDE is always crying over the silliest little thing.

harangue 1. (n.) a ranting speech *We endured the harangue of the hotel manager about us gluing the furniture to the ceiling.* 2. (v.) to give such a speech He continued to harangue us even after we explained the glue would eventually weaken and the furniture would fall. Can you imagine?

calamity (n.) terrible event *September 11ᵗʰ, 2001 was one of the worst calamities in U.S. history.* Calamity Jane was always terrible and frightening. Disaster followed her.

ominous (adj.) foreshadowing evil, spooky *The horror writer terrifies me with his ominous text.* I always found meditation spooky….OOOOOMmmmmOOOMmm

admonish (v.) to criticize, to warn *Steve admonished me not to drop the flaps at too high a speed.* Couldn't think of a good mnemonic here. Got one? Send it to me!

deplore (v.) sorrow, disapproval, negative assessment *We deplored the terrible conditions in the apartment, and vowed to clean it up ourselves.* I deplore a dirty floor.

blemish (n.) an imperfection, flaw, mark on an otherwise perfect surface *The beautiful black piano was blemish-free.* When it comes to nationalities, the FLEMISH aren't perfect.

NOTES

Practice Sentence Completion Questions

For full methodology – see page 19 of this manual

Sentence Completions Set 1

1. The managers listened to the claims about the new program with -------, but the demonstration of the program was so ------- that it won them over.
   (A) enthusiasm … comprehensive
   (B) skepticism … convincing
   (C) excitement … lackluster
   (D) apathy … routine
   (E) hesitation … inconclusive

2. Because the long-time player took a contract with the city's rival team, his former teammates called him a -------.
   (A) recruit
   (B) strategist
   (C) raconteur
   (D) traitor
   (E) moron

3. The information given was not adequate; the parties asked the lecturer to ------- on the uses.
   (A) fathom
   (B) elaborate
   (C) demystify
   (D) ramble
   (E) misconstrue

4. Although Dean Koontz is a mainstream popular American author, in interviews he has said he sees his role in literature as -------.

(A) garrulous

(B) peripheral

(C) egocentric

(D) domineering

(E) grandiose

5. Although the band leader receives compliments on his music repeatedly, almost -------, it is always pleased by such enthusiastic encouragement.

(A) tenuously

(B) staunchly

(C) singularly

(D) incessantly

(E) inimitably

6. Tarissa complained that John ------- too quickly when they were instructed to move by the rude waiter; instead of responding strongly, he complied without protest.

(A) remonstrated

(B) capitulated

(C) compromised

(D) interceded

(E) equivocated

Sentence Completions Set 2

1. As the name suggests, a geochronologist is a person who ------- terrestrial materials to determine their -------.
   (A) combines ... sequence
   (B) gathers ... display
   (C) analyzes ... date
   (D) examines ... excavate
   (E) studies ... synthesize

2. Nicholas has ------- dreams of one day becoming president of the United States.
   (A) grandiose
   (B) reticent
   (C) supercilious
   (D) marginal
   (E) pernicious

3. Contemporary Native American sculpture combines traditional carving techniques with current methods and ideas; therefore, it ------- a Native American practice while -------- a modern cultural identity.
   (A) invalidates ... manifesting
   (B) disregards ... investigating
   (C) reappraises .... dissolving
   (D) supercedes ... negating
   (E) reaffirms ... fashioning

4. Some authors create their works for artistic reasons, but the money lures many since writing popular fiction can be very -------.
   (A) altruistic
   (B) arcane
   (C) lucrative
   (D) ascetic
   (E) promiscuous

5. The salesman was known for both his ------- and his ------- ; he lied frequently, but did so with much charm and flair.
    (A) ambivalence … extravagance
    (B) duplicity … panache
    (C) evasiveness … irascibility
    (D) mendacity … corruption
    (E) brashness … charisma

6. The Brazilian coastline is diverse and lengthy; it varies in makeup from arid to tropical, and ------- for hundreds of miles.
    (A) participates
    (B) dilapidates
    (C) swaggers
    (D) perplexes
    (E) meanders

Sentence Completions Set 3

1. After seeing the movie for the third time, Spencer felt he had the plot completely -------.
(A) mesmerized
(B) stupefied
(C) figured
(D) spent
(E) defied

2. Geo feared his six month break from playing the guitar would cause his musical skills to -------.
    (A)   disseminate
    (B)   align
    (C)   atrophy
    (D)   develop
    (E)   rectify

3. Never at a loss for words, Cassandra was quite -------; this was only surpassed by her pleasant manner; she was also very -------.
    (A) reticent … dreamy
    (B) garrulous … egregious
    (C) loquacious … charming
    (D) tedious … erratic
    (E) talkative … pugnacious

4. Henry's ------- was starting to annoy his co-workers; his inability to make a decision and stick to it was driving them nuts.
    (A) solicitation
    (B) rejuvenation
    (C) admonishment
    (D) professionalism
    (E) vaccilation

5. Josefina had put on so much weight in the past month even though she had told her mother she was dieting; her mother suspected her description of her diet was -------.
    (A) scurrilous
    (B) facetious
    (C) tremulous
    (D) surreptitious
    (E) mawkish

6. The location of the bridge according to the map was obviously -------; the soldiers could not find it when they searched the designated area.
    (A) parsimonious
    (B) skewed
    (C) simpatico
    (D) garrulous
    (E) superstitious

Sentence Completions Set 4

1. Juliette and Luca were not allowed to play in the backyard, since their homework efforts were considered ------- by their mother.
   (A) fortified
   (B) substandard
   (C) mortified
   (D) precious
   (E) tenacious

2. This season's flu is particularly ------- and leaves its victims -------; often unable to climb out of bed in the morning.
   (A) benign … exhausted
   (B) mild … incapacitated
   (C) harmless … energized
   (D) debilitating … lethargic
   (E) popular … revitalized

3. The tsunami ------- the village, for not even a single structure remained standing.
   (A) preserved
   (B) reiterated
   (C) debunked
   (D) razed
   (E) salvaged

4. The new release of *The Whining Mill* was condemned by critics as ------- ; another version that brought nothing new to the work.
   (A) profound
   (B) quixotic
   (C) novel
   (D) hackneyed
   (E) innovative

5. During the 1980's, the airline industry was on the verge of collapse; only a government ------- saved it by providing a much needed ------- of cash.
   (A) allowance ... emanation
   (B) endorsement ... alimony
   (C) endowment ... emission
   (D) censure ... influx
   (E) subsidy ... infusion

6. Some think the dolphin is a fish, but this is a ------- since it is a mammal.
   (A) misnomer
   (B) conduction
   (C) precipice
   (D) portmanteau
   (E) slant

7. While writing his poetry, Robert Frost often isolated himself in a one room cottage; he did not live the life of ------- however, as he made frequent visits to the nearby village for supplies and to socialize.

    (A) a miscreant

    (B) an exhibitionist

    (C) a recluse

    (D) an ideologue

    (E) an iconoclast

8. We were thrilled by the tour of the museum offered by the ------- who was knowledgeable and gregarious.

    (A) docent

    (B) postulant

    (C) nymph

    (D) dictator

    (E) plebe

NOTES

Practice "Vocabulary in Context" Questions

On many standardized tests, there will not be so many questions about "meanings" of words. Here's how they show up.

The following passage is excerpted from the novel, <u>The Whining Mill</u>, written in 2012. In this except, the protagonist is waking from an attack by the antagonist.

My head was still killing me. That was real, and I was fully awake now. I mean, I did not have the kind of headache that I get when I have a bit too much to imbibe the night before – no – this was the kind that made me wonder how the human body was constructed. Nothing should hurt this much. The pain was mixed with the relief I now

5 felt that I had dreamed the most dismal path my life could have taken, and I had not yet destroyed everything I had worked so hard for. I was rip-roaring mad now.

I looked up and for a moment and again had no idea where I was. I felt pressure on my chest, and saw a ceiling beam (or what my non-carpenter mind thought was such) lying across my chest. I felt pressure, but my mind was slowly clearing, and I was calm.

10 The mill. I remember.

One of my best features, if you will permit me, is extreme equanimity in the face of unusual situations. This was serving me well here, as I did not panic. I slowly took stock. I flexed my feet, yes; they were still there and still connected. My arms felt okay as well. This beam that lay across my chest was a bit of a problem, for as I breathed I

15 felt it pressing against me harder. Where the heck had that come from?

My headache eased as I forcibly relaxed and breathed regularly and deeply. I tried to shimmy back a bit, but I could not move. The beam had me pinned. I looked from side to side, but could see nothing of interest or value. I felt, though. I felt a mix of emotions powerfully washing over me. I felt the urge to simply relax and let the

20 emotions take me, but a warning bell sounded somewhere inside my mind and derailed this train of thought. I forced myself to relax again and tried to decipher the emotions.

Slowly, surely, the feelings began to take shape. As I was attempting to mentally label them, I felt light and warmth from behind my head.

11. In line 2, the word "imbibe" most nearly means

(A) drink
(B) salute
(C) ignore
(D) use
(E) defray

12. In line 5, the word "dismal" most nearly means
(A) laconic
(B) garrulous
(C) sad
(D) dangerous
(E) perturbed

13. In line 13, the word "equanimity" most nearly means
(A) anger
(B) resolution
(C) certitude
(D) calmness
(E) mendacity

14. In line 17, the word "shimmy" most nearly means

(A) sing
(B) escape
(C) slide
(D) foray
(E) clean

15. In line 21, the word "decipher" most nearly means
(A) anticipate
(B) extend
(C) encode
(D) fortify
(E) figure

Some Other Fun Vocabulary Questions

For these questions, choose the word (or words) that make the sentence correct.

1) Alex took Cody for a walk, but the dog was so _____ they returned to the house early. Nothing seemed to work to control this dog!
    A) pestiferous
    B) docile
    C) indolent
    D) preposterous
    E) obstreperous

2) Hoping to make it home before the ice cream melted, the trio jumped into the convertible and _____ loudly with mirth and glee as they sped away.
    A) candled
    B) chortled
    C) exasperated
    D) fenneled
    E) procrastinated

3) I couldn't believe it when my wife told me I was moving around in my sleep; I had never _____ hereto forthwith.
    A) lollygagged
    B) somnambulated
    C) adumbrated
    D) flouted
    E) personified

4) Jake and his brother were running a (an) _____ operation that absolutely no one knew about.
A) congealed
B) intricate
C) covert
D) wistful
E) extemperous

5) At the house on Kilburn road, the smoke detector's _____ beeping was driving us mad.
A) forlorn
B) astute
C) pernicious
D) incessant
E) pugnacious

6) Hoping to fool the auditor, Oscar gave the person a (an) _____, in the hopes the records would not show anything wrong with whomever had that name.
A) doppelganger
B) protrusion
C) filcher
D) alias
E) carnivore

7) He had said it was an issue; his _____ to do things counterproductive was causing many problems in his life.

A) terseness

B) openness

C) paucity

D) propensity

E) magnanimousness

8) When Sydney tried to get Sloane out of the hot tub, Sloane was _____ that it was NOT time to leave yet!!!

A) pernicious

B) volatile

C) prescient

D) garrulous

E) adamant

Answers appear later in this manual.

NOTES

Answers to Sentence Completion Questions

Sentence Completion Set 1

1. In the first blank we want something like "caution" or "hesitation", the second blank "great" "awesome" Answer choice (B) is correct.
2. We want "traitor" or "turncoat" or something negative Answer choice (D) is correct.
3. We need "expand" "say more about" Answer choice (B) is correct.
4. Tough one. We need "not mainstream", or "on the side" Answer choice (B) is correct
5. We need "repeatedly" or "lots of times" or "all the time" Answer choice (D) is correct.
6. We need "gave in" or "laid down" Answer choice (B) is correct.

Sentence Completion Set 2

1. First blank we need "studies", second blank "time, age" Answer choice (C) is correct.
2. We need "big" "large", answer choice (A) means exactly that.
3. First blank we want "preserve" or "celebrate", we're not sure, second blank we need "showing" "displaying" Answer choice (E) is correct.
4. We need "money making" Answer choice (C) means exactly that.
5. In the first blank we need "lying" and in the second, "charm." Answer choice (B) is correct.
6. Tough one. We need "exists" or "runs" . Answer choice (E) is correct.

Sentence Completion Set 3

1. We need "figured out" "reasoned" Answer choice (C)
2. "Go down" "lessen" "get worse" Answer choice (C) means exactly that. The word is often used with muscles when someone is injured and cannot exercise.
3. First blank "talkative" second blank "nice, really nice" Answer choice (C) is correct. Did you choose B? Egregious means "really bad"
4. We need "not able to make decisions". Answer choice (E) means exactly that – to go back and forth.
5. "Bull" or "a lie" in the blank. Answer choice (B) is it.
6. "wrong" or "inaccurate" Answer choice (B) is correct.

Sentence Completion Set 4

1. "Not good enough" "not adequate" in the blank. Answer choice (B) is correct.
2. First blank "nasty" "bad" "powerful" second blank "tired" "can't get out of bed" Answer choice (D) is correct.
3. "Destroyed" Answer choice (D) is correct.
4. "Nothing new" Answer choice (D) is correct.
5. "helping thing" first blank – "giving of" second blank. Answer choice (E) is correct.
6. "wrong thing" Answer choice (A)
7. "a person without other people" "alone person" "isolated person" Answer choice (C) is correct.
8. "tour guide" – tough vocabulary here. (A) a docent is one who gives tours of museums.

Answers to Vocabulary in Context Questions

This manual is in no way an exhaustive study of Critical Reading passages. The passage you read is there to give you an idea of how the questions are asked. Many standardized exams feature these types of passages, practice them!

11. Imbibe means (A) to drink

12. Dismal means (B) sad

13. Equanimity means (D) calmness

14. Tricky one. Did you say escape? No, it's (C), slide

15. Decipher means (E), figure

Answers to Some Other Fun Vocabulary Questions

1) obstreperous E) disobedient or poorly behaved
2) chortled B) a short chuckle or laugh
3) somnambulated B) to walk in one's sleep
4) covert C) hidden, secret
5) incessant D) constant, unending, usually with a negative connotation
6) alias d) name used to hide one's true identity
7) propensity D) a tendency towards something
8) adamant E) insistent in maintaining an opinion or position

Alphabetical Index

About The Author

The author teaches and tutors the SAT and ACT tests in the New York City and Long Island areas. He is the author of six non-fiction books for test preparation. Dave is known for his effective and accessible style, and his students enjoy tremendous score gains using his methods. Schools, clubs, academies and learning centers use Dave's methods through the combination of Teacher's Edition/Student Workbooks. The author teaches seminars on his methods, and he conducts training for instructors/tutors who wish to master this methodology.

Author's Website – http://www.thetutormonster.com

Made in the USA
Las Vegas, NV
28 February 2024

86458520R00101